HEAL YOURSELF
COOKBOOK

Grain-Free, Sugar-Free, Hassle-Free Recipes for Busy Families

ASHLEIGH **ZYROWSKI** & DR. NICK **ZYROWSKI**

DEDICATION:

This cookbook is dedicated to our wonderful children.

TABLE OF CONTENTS

I LOVE TO COOK

I LOVE TO EAT

MEET ASHLEIGH

If you've picked up this book, you are searching for a way to bring comforting, delicious, real food to your family in a way that is free from preservatives, artificial colors/flavors, wheat, gluten, sugar, and hydrogenated oils. Every dish in this book has been tested on children under five (including my own), family, friends, doctors, and other guests.

Let me share a bit about myself and why I am so passionate about sharing hassle-free, real-food recipes with the world.

I am a wife and a mother of two. My husband is a doctor who coaches high performers on how to sustainably and naturally reach a new level of health and vitality. Many of the recipes in this book were created to help his NuVision Excel patients with their meal planning. Using ingredients that promote health and healing in the body, I was able to develop delicious meals that heal the body. Each recipe uses simple ingredients and can be prepared quickly, without fancy kitchen tools. My desire is to make cooking healthy, easy, fast, and tasty!

Personally, I spend more time in the kitchen than any other room of the house. There are two honest reasons why:

1. I love to cook.
2. I love to eat.

In fact, some of my earliest childhood memories are ones of my mom and I cooking together. Growing up, I was lucky to always have home-cooked meals. I loved baking, and sharing those creations with others. In high school, friends would request my chocolate chip cookies. In college, I would invite our friends and neighbors over for a spaghetti dinner. Food was therapeutic for me; it relaxed me to cook and bake, and sharing it with others brought joy and lasting memories.

When I got married to my husband, Dr. Nick Zyrowski, we ate as most Americans do – bagels for breakfast, sandwiches for lunch, and more carbs for dinner. Our diet was rich in bad fats, sugar, and carbohydrates, and low in quality protein, green vegetables, and good fats.

While pursing his doctorate degree, we were exposed to a variety of different dietary and nutritional theories. But what really had our gears turning was this persistent question:

What does the human body require to express health?

Like an automobile, what you put into your body matters. The maintenance, waxing, carpet cleaning, proper oil, and fuel are all necessary for your car to last. How much more so for your body!?

After discovering what it takes to heal our bodies and express health from within, we quit the Standard American Diet cold turkey. Like most people, we first asked ourselves:

"What can we eat?"

I viewed this challenge as an opportunity to re-create some of our favorite dishes in a way that was nourishing to our bodies. I wasn't going to eat a salad everyday for dinner! What resulted was a three-ring binder of my favorite go to recipes. I had chicken scratch all over them, notes of changes and modification, substitutions and more. Ultimately, it was my kitchen bible.

As Dr. Zyrowski began coaching high performing individuals with NuVision Health Center, the biggest challenge was helping his clients admit or understand that poor dietary choices puts them in a club which no one wants to belong – one in which millions of Americans suffer from life-threatening diseases. Americans have more degenerative diseases than any other country in the world; 1 out of 2 people die of heart disease, and 1 out of 3 people will develop cancer. We're a mess. It's not just genetics at work here. In places like Okinawa and Indonesia, people not only live longer than Americans; they live their lives free of degenerative diseases. When these people move from their native lands and begin eating as Americans eat, and doing as Americans do (disrupted sleep schedule, lack of exercise, high stress lives, etc.), they develop the same diseases we do. Therefore, it's what we do that defines our health more than genetics. For more info on this, read this article on epigenetics: http://nuvisionexcel.com/?p=2508

Our bodies do not need help healing; they just do not need interferences. Toxins in our food and lives are these interferences that disrupt our genetic expression. Because of this, my husband is on a mission to help people reclaim their health and live with vitality. But the problem he often faces is helping people learn how to prepare healthy meals for themselves and their families.

We believe in food as medicine, and know that by adjusting your diet and lifestyle, you too can wake in the morning refreshed and energized without stimulants, have clarity of mind, feel good all the time, and look your best every day.

This book contains:
- Meals prepared with fresh, real food ingredients, and void of all additives, preservatives, and chemicals.
- No crazy ingredients; everything can be found with minimal searching. For anything that may not be at your local grocery store, check the resources page (page 15) for easy ordering.
- No complicated cooking terms; everyone can use this book. You do not need to know much about cooking to follow these recipes.
- No fancy gadgets; there's no tools or devices you have to buy to make the amazing recipes in this book.
- Simple recipes with dynamic flavor that promote true health within your body.

Food should taste GOOD. Today, food is still therapeutic for me – I'm enjoying creating new, fun and healing recipes and sharing them with those I love. I know you're going to enjoy bringing your family together with meals from my Heal Yourself Cookbook.

Yours in Health,
Ashleigh Zyrowski
P.S. Share your food memories with me on instagram @nuvisionexcel.

NOTE FROM
DR. NICK ZYROWSKI

Heal Yourself Cookbook couldn't have been released at a better time. It's absolutely crucial that everyone gets their hands on this book and starts making strides towards better health, ultimately a better life.

The reason I say this is because people are sick and dying from absolutely preventable health problems, more today than ever before. The black plague killed 30% of Europe. Chronic illnesses are now killing 80% of the industrial world. 1 out of 2 people die of heart disease, and 1 out of 3 people will develop cancer. An absolutely indisputable fact is that the greatest determinant on whether you'll get sick or stay well is your lifestyle.

It is no secret that most people make very poor dietary choices every day. Most people were raised eating a poor diet and now raise their own families on junk food. The average individual doesn't know any better. It was through my own health challenges that I became aware of another world, one of eating right and taking care of yourself.

Now that I know the devastating effects that toxic food/poor quality food has on the human body, I can't bring myself to eat it, and I certainly wouldn't feed it to my own family.

Each and every person has an amazing genetic potential to thrive. This genetic potential needs the proper building blocks. Every meal that you eat becomes part of you, and that is why eating good quality, nutritious, energizing food is so important.

My wife has been making incredible meals for quite sometime; meals that are designed to heal you and not drive inflammation, sickness, and disease. Every meal is specifically made with ingredients that meet these guidelines. Let's discuss what these guidelines are and why they are imperative in order to heal your body.

HEAL YOURSELF GUIDELINES

REMOVE SUGAR

Removing sugar is by far the hardest thing to change, but is vitally important. The average American consumes 53 teaspoons (or half a pound) of sugar per day. That might seem impossible. But consider sodas, juices and cereals. Or what about the sugar added in canned soups, sauces, lunchmeat, yogurt, and spices? Refined sugar is in nearly all packaged foods, even those labeled "healthy", "natural" or "gluten free".

If you're not accustomed to reading labels, then this may come as a shock to you. Why would sugar be in your canned tomatoes? Sugar is cheap and addictive, making it the perfect additive to nearly every boxed food in the grocery store today. And now it comes in a variety of forms: sugar, sucrose, high fructose corn syrup, malt, barley, dextrose, brown rice syrup, etc.

If you've already tried making healthier choices, and are choosing "organic" brands, don't be fooled. Organic sugar, honey, maple syrup, and cane juice, while less processed, are still sugar and have the same negative impact on your body.

If you are a vibrant, healthy individual, then a bit of natural sugars (like honey or maple syrup) will not harm you, and is fine in moderation. However, this book is about healing yourself with foods. Sugar is not a healing substance, and let's discover why.

Sugar is, plain and simple, a toxin. Like all toxins, your body is constantly trying to rid it from the bloodstream. It elevates blood sugar and insulin, causing excessive free radical damage and hormonal imbalances, leading to premature aging and illness. It drives inflammation throughout the body, which is at the heart of 98 percent of disease.

We all have between 100 and 10,0000 cancer cells in our bodies at any given time. Cancer cells utilize sugar as their primary fuel, so robbing them of their number one food choice (sugar) is a great natural and free preventative mechanism for stopping the spread of cancer cells.

As if all of that wasn't reason enough to avoid it, if you avoid sugar, you'll do your waistline a favor. Sugar is the principal dietary cause of the obesity epidemic. Fat is not what makes you fat; it's the sugar that turns into fat.

SUGAR TO AVOID:
Sugar, sucrose, high fructose corn syrup, malt, barley, dextrose, brown rice syrup, cane juice, honey, maple syrup, dates, molasses, agave nectar, maltodextrin. Read labels and avoid anything ending in an –ose.

HIDDEN SOURCES OF SUGAR TO REMOVE:

Soft Drinks: Choose sparkling water instead (like La Croix).
Fruit Drinks: Choose to flavor your water with lemons or limes.
Mayonnaise: Grapeseed Vegenaise is a great substitute.
Ketchup: Choose a xylitol sweetened ketchup (Nature's Hollow) or make your own.
Rice milk: Choose unsweetened almond, cashew, or coconut milk
Yogurt: Choose a plain, unsweetened yogurt from grass-fed cows (like Kalona Supernatural) or coconut yogurt (like So Delicious).

SWEETENERS WE RECOMMEND: Stevia and sugar alcohols like xylitol or erythritol.

REMOVE GRAINS

The truth: you have been thoroughly misled when it comes to conventional dietary advice. Most dietary guidelines have been massively distorted by the very corporations that profit from the obesity epidemic – the processed food industry.

If you take a look at the "food pyramid", you'll notice that grains are firmly nestled as the base of a healthy diet. Even diabetes organizations promote carbohydrates as a major component of a healthy diet—even though grains break down to sugar in your body, which leads to insulin resistance, which is the cause of type 2 diabetes in the first place.

The sad truth is that grain consumption, especially in the forms found today, do spike our insulin production, which throws a wrench in hormone production and leads to inflammation. Our bodies simply can't handle the insulin requirements with the carb load we consume.

But grains are healthy, right? Through the grain production, the bran and germ are stripped out, leaving very little of the minuscule nutritional value the grain had to begin with. When ground into flour, the resulting high-starch food is biologically similar to consuming pure table sugar.

As if that wasn't bad enough, grains are high in phytic acid (a mineral blocker), gluten, (break down the microvilli in your small intestines, leading to Leaky Gut Syndrome), and lectins (don't break down in the gut and leech into your blood stream, leading to food sensitivities).

Grains are not healthy and, in most cases, are toxic to the body. I know it may seem daunting to avoid all grains. Trust me: I used to live on them too. But once you make the switch, and your body gets to live on real food for fuel, you'll realize how great you can feel. You'll watch the pounds fall off, and you'll regain energy you thought belonged only to the youth. Every recipe in this book is grain free, so relax knowing you can consume every meal in this cookbook.

GRAINS TO AVOID: Pasta, pastries, desserts, bread, rolls, crackers, white potatoes, corn, rice, oats, barley, rye, tapioca, spelt, amaranth, sprouted grains, millet, and any forms of "whole grains".

EAT GOOD FATS

All fats are not created equal. The media has trained most of us to think that all fat is bad. Fats are confusing for many people, preventing them from making sound dietary decisions.

Our Western diet is burdened by high levels of omega 6 fatty acids and trans fats, and is lacking in heart-healthy, artery-protecting omega 3 fats. Poor quality fats, like the "franken-fat" trans fat, should be avoided at all cost. But what about the other fats?

Fats are composed of different mixes of fatty acids, and some are good or even essential for survival. Your brain is made of 60% fat. Each one of our cells is surrounded by a lipid (fat) bi-layer. It is therefore necessary to consume good, healthy fats for good neurological health and proper cell function.

Saturated fats have been wrongly demonized in the later half of the 1900s. Saturated fat has been shown to raise "good" (HDL) cholesterol and change the pattern of your "bad" (LDL) to a more favorable pattern. Saturated fat is not associated with a greater risk of heart disease. A study released by Harvard University concluded, "greater saturated fat intake is associated with less progression of coronary atherosclerosis whereas carbohydrate intake is associated with a greater progression." What this is saying is that when you remove saturated fat from your diet, and replace it with high-glycemic carbohydrates, you're actually increasing your risk for heart disease.

Other research shows that omega-6 fats (or vegetable oils) are pro-inflammatory. For years, we've been told to use vegetable oils (like canola oil and margarine) instead of animal fats (like lard and butter). Recent studies confirm that vegetable oils are turning out to be worse than the original saturated animal fats. In fact, the reason that low fat diets work is because they reduce omega-6 fats, not because they reduce saturated fats.

Saturated fats are solid at room temperature, and are found in butter, cheese, meat, and coconut oils. Keep in mind to choose animal meat and animal products from grass-fed/free-range/wild-caught sources. More on this in the Eat Good Meats section below.

Mono-saturated fats are good fats that are liquid at room temperature, such as in olive oil, macadamia, and avocados. These are known to help lower blood cholesterol and prevent artery clogging.

Polyunsaturated fats are broken down into two categories, omega-6s and omega-3s. Essential fatty acids must be consumed in your diet, as your body does not manufacture them. ALA, EPA and DHA are omega 3 fatty acids that are of specific importance, and can be found in walnuts, flaxseeds, fish, and grass-fed meats.

BAD FATS TO AVOID: Hydrogenated and partially hydrogenated oils, trans fats, commercially raised meat and dairy products, and rancid vegetable oils (canola, cottonseed, soybean, corn, sunflower, safflower, peanut oil, and margarine).

SOME GOOD FATS WE RECOMMEND:
Grass-fed butter: Butter from cows that graze on greens (like Kerrygold butter). It's five times higher in conjugated linoleic acid (CLA) and higher in vitamin E and beta carotene than commercial butter.
Pastured eggs: Grass-fed, free-ranging hens raised on pastures produce eggs with 20 times more healthy omega-3 fatty acids than those from factory-raised hens.
Organic whole milk and cheeses: Choose milk from grass-fed cows that have not been treated with hormones. Avoid pasteurization and homogenization, as this denatures the delicate proteins in the milk. Vat-pasteurization is great, as it is pasteurized at a low temperature, but raw is best. Kalona Supernatural is a great brand for milk and cheeses.
Avocados: Avocados are a super-food, meaning they are very nutrient dense. Avocados are a star in Baked Eggs in Avocados *(page 20)* and Avocado Smoothie *(page 146)*.
Coconut and coconut products: Coconut oil is amazing both internally and externally, and coconut milk is the perfect dairy milk substitute for those with sensitivities. So Delicious is a great brand. Use cold-pressed oils.
Raw nuts and seeds: Avoid roasted nuts, as heating can cause the precious oils to become rancid. Soaking and sprouting provide added benefit but is not vitally important.
More fats in the shopping guide on *page 11*

COOKING TIP: Cook in only coconut oil or Grapeseed oil. While butter and olive oil are great fats, they can easily become rancid when heated.

EAT GOOD MEATS

Feedlot-raised animals are exclusively fed grains in the last half of their lives, and their meat has high concentrates of omega 6 fatty acids, with an omega 6 to omega 3 ratio of 20:1 or higher. This skewed fatty acid ratio is at the heart of a host of ailments, such as heart disease and hormonal imbalances.

Grain-fed cattle have a four to six inches of white fat covering their bodies. Grain-fed poultry and eggs have similar issues. They are overweight, obese, sick, and are commonly given antibiotics and hormones.

Grass-fed and free-range meats are lean, have little external fat, and are rich in fatty acids that are vacant from the Standard American Diet: arachidonic acid, CLA, and the proper omega 6 to omega 3 ratio of 2:1 to 4:1. All are vitally important for brain function and fat metabolism.

Saturated fat has also received a bad rap in the media. However, studies show that saturated fat in grass-fed meat actually prevents heart disease. The saturated fat in quality meats and animal products is critical for brain and cell function.

Wild-caught fish tend to be higher in omega-3 fatty acids and protein, contain very low levels of disease and PCBs, and are free of antibiotics, pesticides, and artificial dyes. Wild-caught fish may contain mercury, which is why we recommend that fish consumption is limited to one to two times per week.

MEATS TO AVOID: Commercially raised meats and their bi-products, even those labeled "all-natural". Avoid all farm-raised fish.

GOOD MEATS WE RECOMMEND: Look for words like organic, free-range, wild-caught, grass-fed, pasture-raised. The best place to find these is farmers markets, natural food stores, direct mail sites like grasslandbeef.com, and developing good relationships with local farmers who raise their animals grazing on greens only.

GENERAL FOOD GUIDELINES

OTHER FOODS TO AVOID

Soy: Most Americans have stressed endocrine systems as it is. Why add more toxic estrogen to the mix?
Processed/Packaged foods: Reading labels is crucial here. Even "gluten free", "all-natural" products can contain artificial dyes, bad oils, starchy flours, and other toxic ingredients.

FRUITS AND VEGETABLES

It is estimated that 70% of the worlds soil is depleted of important nutrients. Fruit and vegetables grown in this soil are also depleted of nutrients, and as you consume them, you too lack proper nutrients in your diet. I can say with certainty, based off lab testing and clinical data that I run, that most people are deficient in multiple essential nutrients.

Another major topic of discussion when you're thinking of purchasing fruits and vegetables is the topic of toxicity. Most standard produce has been sprayed heavily with chemicals to keep off pests. The problem is these chemicals are still on the produce when it comes into your home, and in most cases, become part of the produce. When you consume a food with a toxin on it, you become toxic; simple as that.

If that wasn't enough to worry about, there is the topic of Genetically Modified Organisms (GMO). Yes, I understand the controversy that exists around them. Some say they are safe and some say they are not. Many countries have banned them from entering, and the way I look at it, is that I'm not going to be a science experiment. Avoiding GMO foods is an absolute must for myself, my family and for my patients.

Are you only to buy organic? The answer is no. If organic produce is out of your budget, then here is what you do: Go to farmers markets and get to know some local farmers, gardeners, and buy from them. They may be growing high quality produce without using toxic chemicals on them. They may not have the "organic" certification because it's pricey, but are still growing good, wholesome produce. There is also the option of growing a garden yourself. I know this sounds daunting to many, but it's easier than you think.

If all of this sounds too overwhelming to you, then just stick to buying the "Dirty Dozen" list organic, found here: http://nuvision-excel.com/?p=438

SNACKS

One common problem people have when sticking to a diet is that they don't plan ahead. This problem is compounded by the fact that most people do not eat every meal at home. If you don't bring a meal with you or prepare snacks to have on hand, you're more likely to grab the poor quality "fast food" options.

This is why, at the very least, you should have one to two of the snacks listed below on you if you'll be away from the house for any length of time. This way, you'll be more likely to stick to your diet.

1. Green apples & almond butter
2. Trail mix: take a variety of nuts and seeds and toss together. Add in Lily's Dark Chocolate Chips for those looking for a sweet treat. For an added benefit, soak and dehydrate your nuts and seeds.
3. Hard boiled eggs *(page 54)*
4. Cut vegetables
5. Paleo bars: http://tinyurl.com/paleobars

FOOD SENSITIVITY BADGES

Because everyone is different and we all have different genetics and levels of toxicity, the ways our bodies process foods are going to be different. While one person can eat a bite of eggs and have an immediate allergic response, another can eat an omelet a day and not notice a difference.

The take away – even healthy foods can be toxic to your body if you have an allergy or food sensitivity. This is why we always recommend getting a comprehensive food sensitivities test to understand what foods are creating health within your body and which are causing inflammation. To learn more about testing for food sensitivities, check here: http://nuvisionexcel.com/?p=528

Many of the patients we work with have sensitivities to many of the same things: dairy, eggs, gluten, nuts, and wheat. That's why these are specifically labeled on the upper right corner of each recipe, to help you better navigate which recipes are good for your body specifically. While some of these dishes contain dairy, I've given substitute options wherever possible to accommodate people's unique sensitivities.

SHOPPING GUIDE

FATS		FLOURS
Almonds	Vegenaise	Almond flour
Almond Butter	Fresh and dried	Arrowroot powder
Avocados	herbs & spices	Coconut flour
Butter (Raw, Grass-fed)	Mustard	
Cashews	Pure vanilla extract	**CARBOHYDRATES**
Cashew butter	Unsweetened cocoa	(Consume in moderation)
Chia	powder	Artichokes
Coconut or Flakes	Vinegars	Adzuki Beans
Coconut Milk and		Black Beans
	HIGH FIBER	Chick Peas (Garbanzo)
OIL	**VEGETABLES**	French Beans
Cod Liver Oil	Arugula	Great Northern Beans
Eggs (Pasture Raised)	Asparagus	Kidney Beans
Flax and flaxseed oil	Bamboo Shoots	Leeks
Full Fat Plain Yogurt	Bean Sprouts	Legumes
Grapeseed oil	Bell Peppers	Lentils
Grass Fed Meat	Broccoli	Lima Beans
Hemp	Brussels Sprouts	Mung Beans
Hemp Oil (3 to 1 ratio)	Cabbage	Navy Beans
Macadamia Nuts	Cassava	Okra
Pecans	Cauliflower	Peas
Pine Nuts	Celery	Pinto Beans
Pumpkin seeds	Chicory	Pumpkin
Raw Cheeses	Chives	Split Peas
Sesame	Collard Greens	Squash(acorn,
Sunflower	Coriander	butternut, winter)
Walnuts	Cucumber	Sweet Potatoes
	Eggplant	Tomatoes
	Endive	Turnips
PROTEIN	Fennel	White Beans
Beef (Grass-fed)	Garlic	Yellow Beans
Bison	Ginger Root	Yams
Chicken (Free-Range)	Green Beans	
Duck	Hearts of Palm	**FRUIT**
Eggs (Pasture Raised)	Jalapeno Peppers	(Low GI and high
Goose	Kale	antioxidant)
Lamb	Lettuce	Blackberries
Mackerel (wild caught)	Mushrooms	Blueberries
Mahi-Mahi (wild caught)	Mustard Greens	Boysenberries
Pheasant	Onions	Elderberries
Raw Cheeses	Parsley	Gooseberries
Ricotta Cheese (Organic)	Radishes	Granny Smith Apples
Salmon (wild caught)	Radicchio	Grapefruit
Sardines (oil or water)	Snap Beans	Kiwi
Turkey (Free-Range)	Snow Peas	Lemons
Venison	Shallots	Limes
Whey Protein (Raw,	Spinach	Loganberries
Grass Fed)	Spaghetti Squash	Raspberries
	Summer Squash	Strawberries
CONDIMENTS,	Swiss Chard	
SPICES, AND OTHERS	Turnip Greens	**SWEETENERS**
Bone broth	Watercress	Stevia
Coconut Aminos	Zucchini	Xylitol
Grape Seed Oil		

Tips: Use ORGANIC when possible. Choose raw nuts and cheese, grass fed meat, free range and cage free eggs, and no hormone sources when possible. Avoid farm-raised fish. Use cold pressed oils and avoid hydrogenated or partially hydrogenated oils.

MEAL PLANNER
HEAL
YOURSELF
COOKBOOK

WEEK 1 MEAL PLANNER

	BREAKFAST	LUNCH	DINNER	SNACK
SUNDAY	Sweet Potato Hash *(page 42)*	Chicken Salad in Bell Peppers *(page 76)*	Spaghetti Squash & Meatballs *(page 120)*	Cashew Butter Balls *(page 128)*
MONDAY	Green Smoothie *(page 154)*	Chicken Salad over mixed greens *(page 72)*	Chicken Bone Broth Soup (make enough for lunches) *(page 74)*	Crispy Roasted Chickpeas *(page 52)*
TUESDAY	Leftover Sweet Potato Hash *(page 42)*	Chicken Bone Broth Soup *(page 74)*	Cabbage Rolls *(page 100)*	Zucchini Muffins *(page 134)*
WEDNESDAY	Avocado Shake and Zucchini Muffin *(page 146/134)*	Guacamole with Celery Sticks & Cucumber Slices *(page 56)*	Coconut Chicken Nuggets & Butternut Squash Fries *(page 108/50)*	Egg Nog *(page 152)*
THURSDAY	Berry Parfait with Grainless Granola *(page 22)*	Chicken Bone Broth Soup *(page 74)*	Chop Suey and Egg Drop Soup *(page 106/ 80)*	Coconut Water Popsicles *(page 132)*
FRIDAY	Spinach & Mushroom Scramble *(page 38)*	Berry Chicken Salad with Poppy Seed Dressing *(page 72)*	Easy Broiled Mahi Mahi, Steamed cauliflower and broccoli *(page 112)*	Pumpkin Chocolate Chip Cookies *(page 140)*
SATURDAY	Fiesta Breakfast Bowl *(page 30)*	Chicken nuggets and egg drop soup *(page 108)*	Eggplant & Lamb Ragu *(page 114)*	Leftover Pumpkin Chocolate Chip Cookies *(page 140)*

WEEK 2 MEAL PLANNER

	BREAKFAST	LUNCH	DINNER	SNACK
SUNDAY	Waffles Chicken Sausage *(page 24)*	Balsamic Steak & Artichoke Salad *(page 68)*	Paprika Chicken *(page 116)*	Apple Crumble *(page 126)*
MONDAY	Whey Cool Smoothie *(page 158)*	Chili *(page 84)*	Asian Turkey Wraps *(page 94)*	Mini Cheesecakes *(page 138)*
TUESDAY	Crustless Quiche *(page 26)*	Taco Salad with leftover chili	Beef Bone Broth Stew (make enough for lunches) *(page 70)*	Leftover cheesecakes *(page 138)*
WEDNESDAY	Triple Berry Blast *(page 156)*	Beef Bone Broth Stew *(page 70)*	Sloppy Joes in Lettuce Cups, Zucchini & Summer Squash *(page 118)*	Thai Bacon Wrapped Water Chestnuts *(page 62)*
THURSDAY	Egg "Burrito" *(page 28)*	Greek Tossed Salad *(page 82)*	Beef & Cranberry Skillet *(page 98)*	Chocolate Coconut Mousse *(page 130)*
FRIDAY	Veggie Egg Muffins *(page 44)*	Leftover Greek Tossed Salad *(page 82)*	Cauliflower Fried Rice *(page 102)*	Homemade Ice Cream *(page 136)*
SATURDAY	Sweet Potato Skillet *(page 40)*	Beef & Cranberry Skillet and the Cauliflower Fried Rice *(page 98/102)*	Chicken Fajitas *(page 104)*	Red Velvet Cake *(page 142)*

Resources

To make "Heal Yourself Cookbook" as user friendly as possible, I am including places where you can order ingredients that may not be at your local grocery store.

Almond Flour: http://shop.honeyville.com/blanched-almond-flour.html

Grapeseed Vegenaise: http://tinyurl.com/grapeseedvegenaise

Kalona Supernatural: Available at Fresh Thyme Farmers Market, Hy-Vee, Marianos, Natural Grocers, Whole Foods, natural food co-ops, and independent natural food stores. http://kalonasupernatural.com

Kerrygold Butter: http://tinyurl.com/purebutter

Lentil Noodles: http://tinyurl.com/lentilnoodles

Lily's Dark Chocolate Chips: http://tinyurl.com/o4yosgo

So Delicious Dairy Free Products: http://sodeliciousdairyfree.com

Sugar-free Grass-fed Beef Bacon: http://tinyurl.com/sugarfreebacon

Xylitol Sweetened Ketchup: http://tinyurl.com/xylitolketchup

There are a few tools I use in my kitchen on a regular basis that help make healthy cooking easier and quicker. I've provided links to these tools below:

Cuisinart ice cream maker: http://tinyurl.com/okoczrs

Oil Spritzer: http://tinyurl.com/ostb6qt

Pampered Chef Chopper: http://tinyurl.com/nuuxs82

Vitamix: www.vitamix.com

Zoku Popsicle Molds: http://www.zokuhome.com/

BREAKFAST

ALMOND
FLOUR WAFFLES

 Prep time
7 minutes

 Cook time
varies depending on
waffle maker

 Servings 3-4 waffles,
depending on size
of your waffle maker

 Dairy-Free, Grain-Free,
Sugar-Free

These fluffy, buttery waffles are made without yeast or wheat. Who knew being healthy could taste so heavenly?

🌿 Ingredients

- 1 cup almond flour
- ½ cup arrowroot powder
- 2 teaspoons aluminum-free baking powder
- 1 Tablespoons xylitol
- ¼ teaspoon salt
- 1 pastured egg
- 5 Tablespoons grass-fed butter, ghee, grapeseed oil, or coconut oil
- ½ cup + 2 Tablespoons milk (dairy or nondairy)
- 1 teaspoon lemon juice

Instructions

1. Preheat waffle maker.
2. Mix all ingredients together to create batter.
3. Spray griddle with oil and pour batter into preheated griddle.
   Cook waffle according to your griddle's instructions.
4. Top with homemade whipped cream, butter, and/or berries. Serve warm.

📋 Notes

- Instead of using aerosol oil sprays, get an oil sprizer (page....) like this
- You can make these the night before and reheat them in a toaster oven.
- To make homemade whipped cream, place your mixing bowl and metal whisk in your freezer for 10-15 minutes. Pour 1 cup heavy whipping cream and a pinch of stevia into the mixing bowl and whip until high peaks form when you remove the beater.

BAKED EGGS
IN AVOCADOS

Prep time 5 minutes	Cook time 15-20 minutes	Servings 2 people	Dairy-Free, Nut-Free, Grain-Free, Sugar-Free

You'll see avocados used many times throughout this cookbook. It's one of our favorite super foods due to their nutrient density of healthy fats, fibers, and minerals. Pop these avocados in the oven while you get ready for your day and you'll be rewarded with a satiating breakfast.

 Ingredients

- 2 ripe avocados
- 4 pastured eggs
- Sea salt and pepper to taste
- 2 Tablespoons grass-fed butter or ghee
- Optional Garnishes: Crumbled organic feta cheese, chopped walnuts, salsa, cayenne pepper, fresh chives, cilantro, etc.

 Instructions

1. Preheat oven to 425°F
2. Cut the avocados in half and remove pit. Remove 2 spoonful's of flesh from each half to allow space for an egg. Eat, or reserve for another recipe.
3. Gently crack an egg into each avocado half.
4. Place the avocados in glass or stainless steel baking dish. Cover with foil, and bake for 15 to 20 minutes, or until eggs reach desired doneness.
5. Season, top with ½ tablespoon of butter on each, garnish and enjoy!

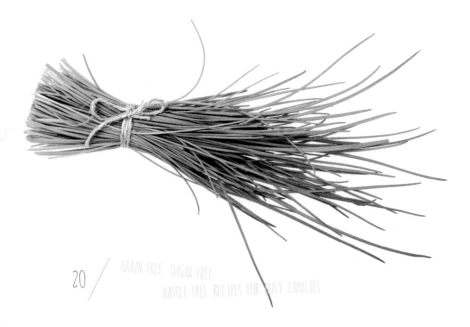

BERRY PARFAITS

Prep time
2 minutes

Cook time
0 minutes

Servings
2 people

Egg-Free, Grain-Free,
Sugar-Free

Parfaits can be a breakfast, snack, or desert in our house. We make them often and top them with this grain-free granola.

Ingredients
- 1 cup unsweetened, full fat yogurt (we like Kalona Supernatural)
- ½ cup organic blueberries, raspberries, and/or chopped strawberries
- 2 Tablespoons grain-less granola

Layer ingredients in two bowls and serve immediately.

SUBSTITUTIONS: You can use any quality unsweetened yogurt. There are many good grass-fed dairy yogurts (like Kalona Supernatural) or dairy-free yogurts. Be sure to watch for added ingredients, like sugar or carrageenan. A more cost-effective solution is to make your own dairy or non-dairy yogurt at home.

Grain-free Granola
- ½ cup whole organic flax seeds
- ½ cup sunflower seeds
- ¼ cup hemp seeds
- ½ cup raw organic nut of choice (almonds, cashews, walnuts, macadamia)
- ½ cup coconut flakes, unsweetened
- ½ teaspoon cinnamon

Instructions
1. In a high powered blender or food processor, combine flax seeds, sunflower seeds, hemp seeds, nut of choice, and coconut flakes. Process until ingredients are reduced to a chunky, grain-like consistency (about 30 seconds).
2. Stop motor. Scrape down to loosen mixture in bottom of blender or bowl, if necessary. Add cinnamon and process a few more bursts until blended.
3. Scoop out and serve with yogurt or with milk of choice for a cereal alternative.

CHICKEN APPLE
BREAKFAST SAUSAGE

 Prep time
10 minutes

 Cook time
20-25 minutes

 Servings
4 people

 Dairy-Free, Egg-Free, Nut-Free,
Grain-Free, Sugar-Free

This sausage recipe is free from sugar, nitrates, and preservatives, which are found in many of the store-bought sausages. Not only can you control the ingredients, you can make them at a fraction of the cost (especially if you grind your own chicken which can easily be done in a high speed blender). Use this recipe to make sausage patties or as a ground sausage for recipes like Sweet Potato Breakfast Skillet (page 40)

Ingredients

- 1 pound ground free-range chicken
- ½ cup onion, finely diced
- ½ organic granny smith apple, finely diced
- 2 Tablespoon ghee or coconut oil
- 1 teaspoon poultry seasoning

- 1 teaspoon garlic powder
- 1 teaspoon parsley
- ¼ teaspoon pepper
- ¼ teaspoon sea salt
- 1/8 teaspoon allspice

 Instructions

PATTIES PREP

1. Preheat oven to 425°F. Line a baking sheet with parchment paper and set aside.
2. Heat a skillet to medium heat with ghee or coconut oil. Add onion and apple and cook until onion and apples are soft. Remove from heat.
3. In a separate bowl, combine onions, apples, chicken, and seasonings together. Form mixture into patties about 3 inches in diameter and ½ inch thick and place on the parchment paper.
4. Bake in the preheated oven for 15-20 minutes, or until no longer pink.

GROUND SAUSAGE PREP

1. Heat a skillet to medium heat with ghee or coconut oil. Add onion and apple and cook until onion and apples are soft.
2. Add chicken and all spices to the onion mixture and continue cooking until meat is no longer pink, stirring frequently.

Notes

You can store the sausage patties in the refridgerator until you are ready to serve. To reheat, simply heat a skillet over medium heat, add a little coconut oil, and let them sizzle away for about 2 minutes on each side until browned to preference. Since they were already fully cooked in the oven, there's no need to worry about doneness. They can also be frozen for later use.

CRUST-LESS BACON AND CHEESE QUICHE

 Prep time
10 minutes

 Cook time
40 minutes

 Servings
8 people

 Nut-Free, Grain-Free,
Sugar-Free

My personal opinion is that bacon and cheese make everything taste better. And this crust-less quiche stars both of those! This quiche is great for brunches or a holiday breakfast and is sure to impress.

Ingredients
- 1 ½ cup sugar-free beef bacon or organic turkey bacon, cooked and crumbled
- 2 cup freshly chopped spinach
- 2 cup chopped mushroom
- 2 cup organic shredded cheddar cheese
- 1 cup organic whole milk (or half and half)
- 7 pastured eggs
- ¼ teaspoon sea salt
- ½ teaspoon pepper
- Coconut oil

Instructions
1. Preheat the oven to 375°F.
2. Grease a pan with coconut oil. Then add the spinach, mushroom, bacon bits, and 1 cup of the shredded cheese in the pan and mix it together.
3. In a separate container, beat the eggs, milk, salt and pepper together with a whisk until blended together well.
4. Pour the egg mixture over the pan of spinach mixture. Put the pan into the oven and bake uncovered for 40 minutes.
5. Once the quiche has finished baking, sprinkle the remaining cheese over the top.

EGG BURRITO

Prep time 2 minutes	Cook time 3 minutes	Servings 1 people	Nut-Free, Grain-Free, Sugar-Free

My favorite thing about this recipe is that it can be thrown together in minutes.
We often make this on busy weekday mornings.

Ingredients
- ½ Tablespoon grass-fed butter
- 2 pastured eggs
- 1 Tablespoon salsa
- 2 Tablespoons organic cheddar cheese, shredded
- 1 Tablespoon guacamole or avocado slices

 ### Instructions
1. Heat butter in an omelet pan over low heat. In a separate bowl, whisk eggs together. Pour eggs into pan.
2. Allow eggs to cook all the way through (no need to flip or stir the eggs). When the eggs are cooked, sprinkle on the cheese. Then, add the salsa down the center of the egg.
3. Carefully remove the egg onto a plate. Fold up both sides and top with a dollop of guacamole or avocado slices.

FIESTA BREAKFAST BOWL

 Prep time
10 minutes

 Cook time
10 minutes

 Servings
4 people

Dairy-Free, Egg-Free, Nut-Free,
Grain-Free, Sugar-Free

This breakfast bowl has all the flavors of a Mexican taco without any of the down-sides. It's full of nutritious ingredients like pastured chicken, bell peppers, salsa, avocados, coconut oil...can you think of a better way to start your day?

 Ingredients
- 1 Tablespoon coconut oil
- 1 small onion, sliced
- 2 organic bell pepper, sliced
- 1 pound ground pasture-raised chicken
- 1 teaspoon dried oregano leaves
- 1 teaspoon chili powder
- ½ teaspoon ground cumin
- ½ teaspoon sea salt
- 1 avocado, sliced
- 2 - 4 Tablespoons salsa

 Instructions
1. In a large skillet, heat the coconut oil. Add onions & peppers to the skillet to soften.
2. When the onions and peppers begin to brown, move them to the edge of the skillet. Add the chicken. Turn the chicken over after a few minutes and break it up into chunks. Continue cooking until the meat is no longer pink. Add the spices, and stir to combine the meat and vegetables.
3. Split the skillet between four bowls. Top each bowl with sliced avocado and salsa.

GRAIN-FREE BISCUITS

 Prep time
5-10 minutes

 Cook time
17-20 minutes

 Servings
12-14 biscuits

 Grain-Free, Sugar-Free

My favorite breakfast used to be southern-style Biscuits and Gravy. When we changed our lifestyle, I knew I had to figure out a way to make a healthy version. I often pair these biscuits with this Sausage Gravy (page 36).

 Ingredients
- 2 cups blanched almond flour
- 1 cup arrowroot powder
- 1 ½ teaspoons baking powder
- ½ teaspoon xanthan gum
- 2 Tablespoons xylitol
- 1 ¼ teaspoons sea salt
- 5 Tablespoons grass-fed butter or ghee, softened
- 2 pastured eggs
- ¼ cup buttermilk (or mix ¼ cup milk with ¼ teaspoon white vinegar)

 Instructions
1. Preheat oven to 400° F.
2. Make the buttermilk. Stir together the milk and vinegar and let stand for 2 minutes.
3. Stir together the dry ingredients until well combined. Add in the butter and cut in with a pastry cutter (or fork) until well blended. Stir in the eggs and buttermilk. If your dough seems a little bit wet, add 1-2 tablespoons of almond flour. You want your dough to be sticky but not wet.
4. Line a 9x13 baking sheet with parchment paper. Roll dough into golf-ball sized balls. Place close together but not touching. Lightly press each biscuit to slightly flatten so they look more like biscuits as opposed to a roll.
5. Bake 17-20 minutes, or until nicely browned.

 Notes
Serve by themselves, with Sausage Gravy *(page 36)*, with a soup, or make an egg and sausage sandwich.

RED & GREEN FRITTATA

Prep time 15 minutes	 Cook time 15-20 minutes	Servings 4 people	Nut-Free, Grain-Free, Sugar-Free

Frittatas are a great way to sneak in a variety of vegetables into your family's diet. Although this specific frittata uses broccoli and red pepper, you can substitute any vegetables you have on hand, ideally leftover cooked vegetables.

 Ingredients

- 6 cups broccoli, cut into bite-sized florets
- 8 pastured eggs
- ¼ teaspoon salt
- ¼ teaspoon pepper
- 1 red bell pepper, diced
- 1 cup raw cheddar cheese, grated
- 4 tablespoon organic Parmesan cheese, grated
- 2 teaspoon coconut oil

Instructions

1. Bring a large pot of water to a boil. Add broccoli and cook until just tender, about 3 three minutes. Drain well.
2. Preheat oven to 350°F. In a large bowl, whisk together eggs, salt, and pepper. Stir in broccoli, red pepper, ¾ cup cheddar cheese, and three tablespoons Parmesan cheese.
3. Heat the coconut oil in a 12" ovenproof frying pan over medium-high heat. Pour the egg mixture into the pan and reduce the heat to medium. Cook for three minutes to set the bottom of the frittata. Sprinkle with remaining ¼ cup cheddar and one tablespoon Parmesan cheese.
4. Transfer the pan to the oven and bake until the frittata is set in the center and slightly puffy, 15-20 minutes. Let cool for five minutes in the pan, then run a spatula around the edges and slide onto a large plate. Cut into wedges and serve.

HEAL YOURSELF COOKBOOK

35

SAUSAGE GRAVY

 Prep time
10 minutes

 Cook time
10 minutes

 Servings
4 people

 Egg-Free, Nut-Free,
Grain-Free, Sugar-Free

Pair this gravy with the Grain-free Biscuits (page 32) for a delicious comfort meal.

Ingredients

- 2 cups organic whole milk (or milk substitute)
- 4 Tablespoons grass-fed butter
- 1/4 cup arrowroot powder
- 1 pound chicken breakfast sausage *(page 24)*
- Sea salt and pepper to taste

Instructions

1. Brown sausage in a frying pan over medium heat until no longer pink.
2. To make a roux, melt butter over low heat (do not let it brown). Whisk in the arrowroot powder until a thick paste forms. Then slowly pour in the milk while whisking. Stir constantly to make sure no clumps form in the gravy. Remove from heat. Add cooked sausage to gravy and stir.
3. Serve over grain-free biscuits.

SPINACH &
MUSHROOM SCRAMBLE

 Prep time
3 minutes

 Cook time
5-7 minutes

 Servings
2 people

 Nut-Free, Grain-Free,
Sugar-Free

The reason I love this recipe is it is so fast, so easy, and full of flavor.

 Ingredients
- ¼ cup chopped mushrooms
- ½ cup chopped spinach
- 1 Tablespoon grass-fed butter
- 4 pastured eggs
- ¼ cup organic feta cheese
- Sea salt & pepper to taste

Instructions
1. In a medium frying pan, melt butter over medium-low heat. Sauté mushrooms until tender, and then add the chopped spinach.
2. Crack eggs into pan and stir frequently until cooked through. Sprinkle with feta cheese and serve.

39

SWEET POTATO
BREAKFAST SKILLET

 Prep time
10 minutes

 Cook time
20-25 minutes

 Servings
6 people

 Dairy-Free, Nut-Free,
Grain-Free, Sugar-Free

As you'll be able to see throughout this cookbook, we love sweet potatoes. Not only do they taste sensational, they are very nutrient dense. Although this takes some prep work, you'll only be using one skillet.

Ingredients
- 2 Tablespoons coconut oil or ghee
- 6 cups sweet potato, peeled and grated
- 1 yellow onion, chopped
- 1 pound chicken breakfast sausage (uncooked)*(page 24)*
- Sea salt and pepper to taste
- 6 pastured eggs
- Sliced avocado (optional)

Instructions
1. Preheat oven to 350° F.
2. Turn stove on medium high heat and melt coconut oil in an oven safe skillet. Add onion and sausage to the skillet and cook until the sausage is cooked through and crumbly.
3. Add grated sweet potato, salt and pepper to onion and sausage mixture. Continue cooking for 3-4 minutes. Sweet potato should still hold its grated appearance and not get mushy. Be sure not to overcook as the mixture will have more cook time in the oven.
4. Turn off heat. With a spoon, create 6 holes in sweet potato and sausage mixture. Crack 1 egg in each hole.
5. Cover and place skillet in oven for approximately 10-15 minutes depending on desired firmness of your egg.
6. To serve, scoop onto a plate and garnish with sliced avocado.

SWEET POTATO HASH

 Prep time
15 minutes

 Cook time
30 minutes

 Servings
4 people

 Dairy-Free, Egg-Free, Nut-Free,
Grain-Free, Sugar-Free

This sweet and savory hash has become a family favorite. We make it for brunches and it is usually the first thing to go. If we have leftovers, they can easily be reheated during the week when we have less time for meal prep.

Ingredients
- 4 sweet potatoes (about 8 cups), peeled and chopped
- 3 organic granny smith apples (about 4 cups), cored and chopped
- 1 sweet onion (about 2 cups), finely chopped
- 1 pound chicken breakfast sausage *(pages 24)*
- 1 teaspoon sea salt (or to taste)
- ½ teaspoon pepper (or to taste)
- 1 teaspoon garlic powder (or to taste)
- 2 Tablespoons coconut oil, divided

Instructions

1. Preheat the oven to 400° F.
2. Place chopped sweet potatoes in two 9 x 13 pans and drizzle with coconut oil and sprinkle with spices to taste. Toss to coat.
3. Roast the sweet potatoes until they are soft but not mushy, about 10 to 15 minutes. Remove from the oven and reserve.
4. While the sweet potatoes are cooking, cook sausage in a medium skillet until browned and cooked through. Add the onions and apples and sauté an additional 5 minutes, or until onions are translucent.
5. Pour this mixture over the sweet potato mixture and add to the oven for an additional 15 minutes or until sweet potatoes are soft and starting to brown.

VEGGIE
EGG MUFFINS

 Prep time
5 minutes

 Cook time
10 minutes

 Servings
12 muffins

 Dairy-Free, Nut-Free,
Grain-Free, Sugar-Free

There are occasions when we have to travel (for business or pleasure) and know there won't be much we want to eat. In those cases, I make these muffins ahead of time and bring them along. You can also make these ahead of time and easily reheat them when you're ready.

 Ingredients
- 1 cup spinach, chopped
- ½ cup organic red bell pepper, diced
- ½ Tablespoon fresh cilantro, chopped (optional)
- ⅛ teaspoon red pepper flakes (optional)
- ¼ teaspoon sea salt
- 9 pastured eggs, beaten
- Avocado or guacamole (serve on the side)

 Instructions
1. Preheat oven to 350° F. Grease a 12 cup muffin pan with coconut oil.
2. In a medium bowl, add chopped spinach, bell pepper, cilantro, red pepper flakes, and sea salt and stir to combine. Evenly distribute veggie mixture into muffin cups.
3. In a separate bowl, beat eggs. Carefully pour beaten egg mixture over veggie mix in cups. Make sure to fill just slightly below rim of cups.
4. Bake muffins for 30 minutes or until eggs have set. Muffins are best served warm, but can be stored in an airtight container in the refrigerator and reheated later.

 Notes
- Feel free to play with the vegetables in this recipe. Just add 1 ½ cups of whatever vegetables you have on hand and adjust the spices to fit your family's preferences.
- Another option is to add cooked and crumbled Chicken Breakfast Sausage to the vegetable mixture.

APPETIZERS & SNACKS

BUFFALO CHICKEN WINGS

 Prep time
5 minutes

 Cook time
45 minutes

 Servings
8 people

Dairy-Free, Egg-Free, Nut-Free, Grain-Free, Sugar-Free

Buffalo Wings are normally a favorite at every party or sporting event. The only problem is – most are covered in an undesirable sauce. These wings start with a better quality meat and are coupled with a super simple and delicious wing sauce.

Ingredients
- 3 pounds pasture-raised buffalo chicken wings
- ½ cup xylitol sweetened ketchup
- 4 Tablespoon grass-fed butter
- 2 Tablespoon Tabasco sauce (or Frank's)
- 1 Tablespoon mustard

Instructions
1. Preheat oven to 425° F. Line two baking sheets with unbleached parchment paper.
2. Line the wings in a single layer on the parchment paper. Bake for 40 minutes, flipping the chicken after 20 minutes.
3. When the chicken is almost done, melt butter in a small saucepan over low heat. Add ketchup, tabasco, and mustard and stir to combine. Taste. For a spicier sauce, add more tabasco. For a tangier sauce, add more mustard. Set buffalo sauce aside.
4. Remove chicken from oven and brush with buffalo sauce. Return to oven for an additional 5 minutes.
5. Serve wings with extra buffalo sauce for dipping.

Notes
You can buy the full chicken wing to save money. Simply cut the chicken wing into drummetts and wingette by cutting at the joint. You can then cut the tip off and use it to make chicken bone broth.

BUTTERNUT SQUASH FRIES

 Prep time
5 minutes

 Cook time
25-30 minutes

 Servings
4 people

 Dairy-Free, Egg-Free, Nut-Free,
Grain-Free, Sugar-Free

What goes better with a burger than some delicious French fries? Unfortunately, most fries are made with starchy white potatoes that are cooked in hydrogenated oils. These fries are full of flavor and go great with Sweet Potato Sliders (page 122) or Coconut Chicken Nuggets (page 108).

Ingredients
- 1 butternut squash
- 1 Tablespoon coconut oil
- Garlic, salt, pepper to taste

Instructions
1. Preheat oven to 425° F. Peel butternut squash and chop into shoestrings.
2. Drizzle lightly with coconut oil, sprinkle with spices, and toss to coat. Spread out into a single layer on two large baking sheets or baking stones. Roast for 25 to 30 minutes, flipping half way through. We like ours starting to brown/blacken.

Notes
Can't find a butternut squash at the store? You can use sweet potatoes instead. Bonus – you don't have to peel sweet potatoes.

CRISPY ROASTED CHICKPEAS

 Prep time
2 minutes

 Cook time
20-30 minutes

 Servings
2 people

 Dairy-Free, Egg-Free, Nut-Free,
Grain-Free, Sugar-Free

There are many variations to this simple, high-protein snack available. The reason we like this one is because it is quick and easy. We frequently eat this in place of popcorn during movies, or prepare them and take them with us while traveling.

Ingredients
- 1 (15 oz.) can chickpeas
- 1 Tablespoons grapeseed oil
- 1/2 teaspoon sea salt
- 1-2 teaspoons spices or herbs, like chili powder, cumin, paprika, rosemary, thyme, etc.

Instructions
1. Heat the oven to 400°F. Line a baking sheet with aluminum foil or unbleached parchment paper.
2. Rinse chickpeas thoroughly under running water. Pat dry with a clean towel.
3. Toss chickpeas, oil, salt and desired spices together until the chickpeas are thoroughly coated.
4. Roast the chickpeas in the oven for 20-30 minutes, stirring once. The chickpeas are done when golden and slightly darkened, dry and crispy on the outside, and soft in the middle.

Notes
- Besides eating these chickpeas as a snack, you can toss them with salads or sprinkle over soup in place of croutons.
- Another option is to toss these with olive oil, xylitol, and cinnamon for a sweeter snack.

HARD COOKED EGGS (EASY TO PEEL)

 Prep time
2 minutes

 Cook time
15 minutes

 Servings
12

 Dairy-Free, Nut-Free,
Grain-Free, Sugar-Free

Hard cooked eggs are an easy, high protein snack to take with you. However, I went years without making them because I hated peeling them. I always lost half of the egg trying to remove the shell. Then I was given a new way to make hard cooked eggs, and now I make them all the time. Make these for snacks, quick breakfast on-the-go, or for a deviled egg appetizer.

 Ingredients
- 1 dozen pastured eggs

 Instructions
1. Allow eggs to reach room temperature. Place a steamer basket in a pan with several inches of water. Bring to a rapid boil.
2. Carefully add the eggs to the steamer basket while the water is boiling. The eggs should be in a single layer only (do not stack the eggs). Cover and steam for 15 minutes.
3. Shut off stove. Remove eggs from the steamer basket and place in ice water for 10 minutes.
4. When cool enough to handle, crack and peel. Store eggs in the refrigerator.

DEVILED EGGS

 Prep time
5 minutes

 Cook time
0 minutes

 Dairy-Free, Nut-Free,
Grain-Free, Sugar-Free

We make deviled eggs every Easter. It's a quick appetizer that's high in protein and rich in flavor.

 Ingredients
- 6 hard cooked eggs, peeled and cut lengthwise
- ¼ cup Grapeseed Vegenaise
- ½ teaspoon dry ground mustard
- ½ teaspoon white vinegar
- ⅛ teaspoon sea salt
- ¼ teaspoon black pepper
- Paprika for garnish

 Instructions
Remove the egg yolks. Place yolks in a small bowl and mash with a fork. Add vegenaise, dry mustard, white vinegar, sea salt, pepper and mix thoroughly. Fill the empty egg whites with the yolk mixture and sprinkle lightly with paprika

GUACAMOLE

 Prep time
25

 Cook time
0 minutes

 Servings
5 people

 Dairy-Free, Egg-Free, Nut-Free,
Grain-Free, Sugar-Free

Fresh guacamole is a fiesta of flavor. This creamy dip tastes fantastic with fresh vegetables, on top of a grilled chicken breast, with eggs, or on a juicy bison burger. Anyway you serve it, this guac is sure to be a hit.

Ingredients
- 4 avocados
- ½ of a jalapeno pepper, seeded and minced
- ¼ cup sweet onion, finely chopped
- 2 Tablespoon fresh cilantro, finely chopped
- ½ Tablespoon lime juice, or to taste
- ¼ teaspoon salt, or to taste
- Optional: ½ cup sun-dried tomatoes

 ### Instructions
Mash everything together, or blend in a food processor/Vitamix until the desire consistency is reached.

MEATBALLS

 Prep time
5 minutes

 Cook time
30 minutes

 Servings
24 meatballs

 Nut-Free, Grain-Free,
Sugar-Free

Our favorite way to eat these meatballs is with spaghetti. We also love having them as appetizers with dipping sauce or in Cream of Mushroom Soup.

Ingredients
- 1 pastured egg
- ½ cup Parmesan cheese (optional)
- ½ cup onion, finely diced
- 1 teaspoon sea salt
- ½ teaspoon pepper
- 1 teaspoon garlic powder
- 1 pound grass-fed beef/bison/venison

 ### Instructions
1. Combine all ingredients together in a bowl. Shape into 1" balls. Arrange meatballs in a baking dish. If using a lean meat, use parchment paper so the meatballs do not stick.
2. Bake meatballs in the oven on 400°F for 30 minutes. Meatballs are done when cooked through.

SUBSTITUTIONS: If you have an egg sensitivity, substitute a flax egg. To make a flax egg, mix three tablespoons of water with one tablespoon of ground flax meal. Allow to sit for 5 minutes to gel, then add to the meat mixture.

SWEET POTATO BISCUITS

 Prep time
10 minutes

 Cook time
22-27 minutes

 Servings
12-14 biscuits

 Dairy-Free, Nut-Free,
Grain-Free, Sugar-Free

Ingredients

- 2 cups sweet potato, cooked and mashed
- 3 Tablespoons coconut flour
- 3 pastured eggs
- 6-8 strips of sugar-free beef or turkey bacon, cooked and crumble
- ¼ cup coconut oil, melted
- ¼ cup chives, diced
- 1 teaspoon aluminum-free baking powder
- ½ teaspoon garlic powder
- Sea salt and pepper, to taste

Instructions

1. Preheat oven to 350°F. Line a baking sheet with parchment paper and set aside.
2. In a large bowl, combine sweet potato, eggs, and coconut oil. Mix well. Add in your coconut flour, baking powder, garlic powder, sea salt, and pepper. Mix well. Finally, add your diced cooked bacon and chives. Mix thoroughly.
3. Using a large spoon, drop your biscuits onto the parchment-lined baking sheet, shaping them as needed. Place in oven and bake for 22-27 minutes.
4. Let the biscuits rest about 5 minutes. Top with grass-fed butter.

Notes

You can use ¼ cup grass-fed butter in place of the ¼ coconut oil.

THAI BACON WRAPPED
WATER CHESTNUTS

 Prep time
5 minutes

 Cook time
12-15 minutes

 Servings
12 people

 Dairy-Free, Egg-Free, Nut-Free,
Grain-Free, Sugar-Free

This appetizer takes little time and little effort but delivers explosive flavor.

 Ingredients
- 1 can whole water chestnuts
- ¼ cup Thai Ginger Lime Marinade *(page 170)*
- 2 slices sugar-free beef or turkey bacon
- Wooden toothpicks

 Instructions
1. Marinate water chestnuts for at least one hour in the refrigerator (or longer for more flavor). Meanwhile, soak toothpicks in water.
2. Slice bacon into fourths.
3. Discard marinade and wrap each chestnut in a piece of bacon and secure with toothpick.
4. Cook 12-15 minutes on 400° F or until bacon is very crispy.

SOUPS & SALADS

BACON CHEDDAR
BROCCOLI SALAD

 Prep time
10 minutes

 Cook time
0 minutes

 Servings
8 - 10 people

 Egg-Free, Nut-Free, Grain-Free,
Sugar-Free

This salad is a fresh addition to any picnic or cookout. You can also add chicken to this salad and it makes a quick and portable meal.

 Ingredients

- 6 cups fresh broccoli florets
- 1 ½ cups shredded cheddar cheese
- ⅓ cup onion, chopped
- 1 ½ cups Grapeseed Vegenaise
- ¼ cup xylitol
- 3 Tablespoons red wine vinegar
- 12 strips of sugar-free beef or turkey bacon, cooked and crumbled
- 1 pound pasture-raised chicken breasts, cooked and diced (optional)

 Instructions

1. In a large bowl, combine the broccoli, cheese and onion. In a small bowl, combine the vegenaise, xylitol and vinegar.

2. Pour over broccoli mixture; toss to coat. Cover and refrigerate for at least 30 minutes. Just before serving, stir in the bacon and chicken (if desired).

 Notes

Save the stalks of the broccoli for a stir-fry or to make your own vegetable broth.

BALSAMIC STEAK & ARTICHOKE SALAD

 Prep time
5 - 10 minutes

 Cook time
10 minutes

 Servings
4 people

 Dairy-Free, Egg-Free, Nut-Free,
Grain-Free, Sugar-Free

This is a quick salad that combines hearty steak, light greens, crisp vegetables, and a flavorful dash of balsamic vinaigrette.

 Ingredients

- 10 ounces top sirloin/rib eye, grass-fed
- 4 cups mixed greens (spinach, arugula, spring mix)
- 1 pint organic cherry tomatoes, halved
- 1 cup canned artichoke hearts, drained
- 4 Tablespoon balsamic vinaigrette *(page 164)*

 Instructions

1. Grill or broil steak until done, approximately 7-10 minutes on each side. Cool and cut into 1" slices.
2. Toss together the greens, tomatoes, and artichoke hearts and arrange on plates. Top with the steak and drizzle with balsamic vinaigrette.

BEEF BONE BROTH STEW

 Prep time
10 minutes

 Cook time
20 - 30 minutes

 Servings
8 people

 Dairy-Free, Egg-Free, Nut-Free,
Grain-Free, Sugar-Free

Bone broth is an ancient healing food. The practice of consuming bone broth has been around for centuries; however most people in the modern world do not utilize this precious food to nourish their bodies. Making it is super simple, and you can either drink it alone, or add grass-fed beef and vegetables to it to make it a comforting and gut-healing meal.

Ingredients
- 2 pounds grass-fed beef sirloin steak, cut into 1" cubes
- 3 Tablespoon arrowroot powder
- 2 Tablespoon coconut oil
- 4 cups beef bone broth (or beef broth)
- 1 onion, sliced
- 5 celery stalks, chopped
- 1 sweet potato, peeled and cubed
- 1 pound zucchini and/or green beans
- 2 teaspoon sea salt
- ½ teaspoon ground thyme
- ¼ teaspoon black pepper
- 4 cloves garlic, mined

Instructions
1. Coat beef with arrowroot. Heat 1 tablespoon oil in a large nonstick skillet or Dutch oven on medium-high heat. Add half of the beef; brown on all sides. Repeat with remaining beef, adding remaining 1 tablespoon of the oil. Return all beef to skillet.
2. Stir in broth and seasonings. Add vegetables; bring to a boil. Reduce heat to low, cover and simmer for 20 minutes or until vegetables are tender.

BERRY CHICKEN SALAD

 Prep time
5-10 minutes

 Cook time
0 minutes

 Servings
2 people

 Dairy-Free, Egg-Free, Nut-Free, Grain-Free, Sugar-Free

This fresh salad tastes amazing with the sweet Poppy Seed Dressing (page 168). You can also toss in almond slices, sunflower seeds, or cubed avocado for additional healthy fats.

 Ingredients
- 1 pound pasture-raised chicken breasts, grilled and sliced
- 1 cup sliced organic strawberries
- 1 cup organic blueberries
- 6 cups greens romaine lettuce, chopped (about 3 hearts)

 Instructions
Toss all ingredients together. Serve with Poppy Seed Dressing.

CHICKEN BONE BROTH SOUP

Prep time 10 minutes	 Cook time 20-30 minutes	Servings 10 people	 Dairy-Free, Egg-Free, Nut-Free, Grain-Free, Sugar-Free

Did your mom make you chicken soup when you were sick? Turns out, there's truth to the old wives tale. Chicken soup is one of the most healing foods for your body. But this is only true when made with bone broth and lots of fresh ingredients. Added bonus: this soup can be made for under $20 and feed 10+ people.

Ingredients

- 14 cups chicken bone broth (or organic chicken broth)
- 4 cups pasture-raised chicken, cooked and diced
- 4 cups onions, diced
- 3 cups celery, diced
- 3 cups zucchini, diced
- 3 cups frozen peas
- 4 cups lentil noodles, cooked (optional)
- 2 teaspoon garlic powder
- 1 teaspoon pepper
- 2 teaspoon sea salt
- 1 bay leaf
- ¼ teaspoon turmeric
- ¼ teaspoon Italian seasoning
- 2 Tablespoon seasoning salt

Instructions

1. Over medium heat, add ¼ cup broth to a bottom of a large pot. Add onions, celery, and zucchini and cook for 5 minutes.
2. Meanwhile, in a separate pot, boil water for lentil noodles. Cook according to package directions. Strain and set aside.
3. Add peas, chicken and spices to vegetable mixture. Stir to combine. Add 14 cups of chicken bone broth to the vegetables. Bring to a boil, then reduce heat to simmer for 20 minutes. When noodles are tender, add to soup and stir to combine. Keep warm until ready to serve.

HOMEMADE SEASONING SALT

Ingredients

- ½ cup sea salt
- 2 Tablespoon xylitol
- 4 teaspoon paprika
- 2 teaspoon garlic powder

- 1 teaspoon garlic salt
- 4 teaspoon onion powder
- 1 teaspoon pepper

Measure all the ingredients into a jar. Place a lid on the jar and shake until well blended.

CHICKEN SALAD

 Prep time
5-10 minutes

 Cook time
0 minutes

 Servings
4 people

 Dairy-Free, Egg-Free, Grain-Free, Sugar-Free

This crunchy salad is full of high-quality protein and good fats   This easily portable lunch can be served alone, on lettuce or spinach, inside an avocado, or on top of cubed red and green peppers.

Ingredients
- 2 cups pasture-raised chicken, cooked and diced
- ½ cup celery, diced
- ½ cup organic green apple, diced
- 2 Tablespoons green onions, chopped
- 1 teaspoon lemon juice
- ½ cup Grapeseed Vegenaise
- ¼ cup walnuts or pecans, coarsely chopped
- Sea salt and pepper to taste

Instructions
In a large bowl, mix all ingredients together until combined. Refrigerate until ready to eat.

CREAM OF MUSHROOM

 Prep time
10 minutes

 Cook time
10 minutes

 Servings
4 people

 Egg-Free, Nut-Free,
Grain-Free, Sugar-Free

Before I understood how to properly nourish my body, I often used canned cream of mushroom soup in recipes. Now that I know how flavorful real mushroom soup can be, I can't imagine ever using canned soup again. Added bonus: it's full of good fats and fresh ingredients, and void of rancid vegetable oils, wheat flour, and soy.

Ingredients
- 2 Tablespoons grass-fed butter
- ¼ cup onions, chopped
- 2 garlic cloves, minced
- 4 cups sliced fresh mushrooms
- 3 Tablespoons arrowroot powder (separated)
- 2 cups organic chicken broth
- 1 cup organic half and half
- ½ teaspoon salt
- ¼ teaspoon pepper

Instructions
1. Melt butter in a large frying pan on low heat. Add in onions, garlic, and mushrooms. Cook until onions are soft.
2. Whisk in 1 tablespoon of arrowroot powder and stir.
3. Add in the chicken broth and heat until slightly thickened while stirring frequently.
4. In a separate bowl, whisk cream with additional 2 tablespoon arrowroot powder and seasonings. Add in cream to soup. Heat to thicken while stirring frequently.

EGG DROP SOUP

 Prep time
5 minutes

 Cook time
5 minutes

 Servings
4 people

 Dairy-Free, Nut-Free,
Grain-Free, Sugar-Free

If you've ever been to a Chinese restaurant in America, then you've likely seen this soup on the menu. Make a super satisfying version at home for a quick and inexpensive meal or appetizer. It has a good amount of ginger, which is an amazing healing spice. Using bone broth is another great way to maximize the nutritional value of this meal.

 Ingredients
- 4 cups organic chicken broth
- 1 teaspoon ground ginger
- 1 Tablespoon coconut aminos
- 3 pastured eggs, beaten
- ¼ cup chopped green onions (about 2 green onions)
- Sea salt and pepper (to taste)

 Instructions
1. Add chicken broth, ground ginger, and coconut aminos to a saucepan; bring to a simmer. Slowly stream in beaten eggs while stirring the soup in one direction. Add sea salt and pepper to taste.
2. Top with green onions and serve.

GREEK TOSSED SALAD

 Prep time
10 minutes

 Cook time
0 minutes

 Servings
4 people

 Dairy-Free, Egg-Free, Nut-Free,
Grain-Free, Sugar-Free

Sometimes the traditional green salad gets boring. That's how I created this recipe. I decided that I'd skip the lettuce and load up on all of my favorite parts of a Greek salad. It has lots of good fats and quality protein to help hold you over to your next meal.

 **Ingredients**

Salad
- 2 organic cucumbers
- 4-5 organic tomatoes
- 1 large organic red bell pepper
- ½ cup red onion
- 1 (15 ounce) can garbanzo beans, rinsed and drained
- Optional Add-ins: olives, feta, cooked chicken

Dressing
- 3 Tablespoon red wine vinegar
- ¼ cup extra virgin olive oil
- 2 teaspoon dried oregano
- ¼ teaspoon sea salt

 Instructions
1. To make the dressing, combine all ingredients in a small bowl and whisk to combine. Set aside.
2. Dice the cucumbers, onion, bell pepper and tomatoes. Combine the vegetables and garbanzo beans in a large bowl. Pour in dressing and any add-ins. Toss to combine.

 Notes
For extra credit, you can soak, sprout, and cook your own garbanzo beans.

HEARTY CHILI

 Prep time
10 minutes

 Cook time
30 minutes

 Servings
4 people

 Dairy-Free, Egg-Free, Nut-Free,
Grain-Free, Sugar-Free

This meal is perfect on a cool winter night. Also try it on top of salad greens for a quick and easy taco salad, or with an organic hot dog for a bun-less chili dog.

 Ingredients

- 1 Tablespoon coconut oil
- ½ onion, chopped
- ½ cup celery, chopped
- 2 cloves garlic, minced
- 1 organic green pepper, chopped
- 1 pound ground buffalo, grass fed beef, or ground turkey
- 2 teaspoon oregano
- 3 teaspoon chili powder
- 2 teaspoon ground cumin
- 1 teaspoon sea salt
- ½ teaspoon pepper
- 2 (15.5 ounce) cans kidney beans, drained and rinsed
- 2 (14.5 ounce) cans organic diced tomatoes
- 1 (15 ounce) can organic tomato sauce

 Instructions

1. In a large skillet, melt oil and sauté onions, celery, garlic, and peppers until onion is translucent, about 3-4 minutes.
2. Add ground meat, oregano, chili powder, and cumin. Continue cooking, stirring frequently for 5-6 minutes.
3. Pour salt and pepper, beans, tomatoes, and sauce into pot. Cover, reduce heat, and simmer for at least 20 minutes (1 hour for best flavor).

MOROCCAN BUTTERNUT SQUASH SOUP

 Prep time
15 minutes

 Cook time
25-30 minutes

 Servings
4 people

 Dairy-Free, Egg-Free, Nut-Free, Grain-Free, Sugar-Free

The sweet butternut squash and the meaty chicken showcase how well sweet and savory flavors play together in this Moroccan dish. For extra credit: make this soup with bone broth for added minerals and healing compounds like collagen, proline, glycine, and glutamine.

 Ingredients

- 1 Tablespoon coconut oil
- 1 onion, chopped
- 2 cups pasture-raised chicken breasts/thighs, chopped
- 1 teaspoon ground cumin
- ¼ teaspoon ground cinnamon
- ⅛ teaspoon red pepper flakes
- 4 cups butternut squash, peeled and cubed
- 2 Tablespoons organic tomato paste
- 4 cups organic chicken bone broth or chicken stock
- ¾ teaspoon sea salt
- ¼ teaspoon dried basil
- 2 zucchini, quartered lengthwise and sliced

 Instructions

1. Heat a large pot over medium heat. Add oil to pan and swirl to coat.
2. Add onion and chicken. Cook for 4 minutes, until chicken is browning on all sides.
3. Add cumin, cinnamon, and red pepper to pan; cook for 1 minute, stirring constantly.
4. Add butternut squash and tomato paste; cook for 1 minute. Stir in chicken broth; scraping pan to loosen any browned bits. Bring to a boil. Reduce heat and simmer for 8 minutes.
5. Stir in salt, basil, and zucchini and cook 5 minutes or until squash is tender.

ROASTED
SWEET POTATO SALAD

|  Prep time
15-20 minutes | Cook time
20-25 minutes | Servings
8 people | Dairy-Free, Egg-Free, Nut-Free,
Grain-Free, Sugar-Free |

This is a fresh twist on the traditional potato salad. Even the most diehard white potato fan will be won over with the burst of color and flavor in this Roasted Sweet Potato Salad. This dish is sure to impress at your next potluck or picnic.

Ingredients
- 12 cups sweet potatoes, peeled and cubed
- 3 Tablespoons coconut oil
- 1 ½ teaspoon sea salt
- Pepper to taste
- 4 stalks celery, chopped
- ¼ cup red onion, diced
- 1 (6 ounce) can black olives, sliced
- ½ teaspoon dried dill
- 1 teaspoon dried parsley
- ¼ teaspoon onion powder
- ⅓ cup Grapeseed Vegenaise
- 1 Tablespoon apple cider vinegar
- Sea salt and pepper, to taste

Instructions
1. Preheat oven to 450°F.
2. Place the sweet potatoes in a large bowl. Add coconut oil, salt, and pepper to taste. Toss to coat.
3. Place the sweet potatoes in an even layer on two parchment-lined baking sheets. Bake for 20-25 minutes, or until potatoes are soft and browned.
4. Meanwhile, mix the salad ingredients in a large bowl. Add cooled sweet potatoes and stir to combine. Adjust seasonings to taste. Chill salad for 1 hour before serving for best taste.

Notes
Salad can be stored in an airtight container in the refrigerator for up to 2 days.

VEGETABLE MINESTRONE SOUP

 Prep time
10 minutes

 Cook time
25 minutes

 Servings
4-6 people

 Dairy-Free, Egg-Free, Nut-Free,
Grain-Free, Sugar-Free

Make this hearty Italian minestrone soup for dinner and enjoy the leftovers for lunch. It's easy to make and can even be made in a crockpot. There's nothing like coming home to a wonderful smelling kitchen. Bon Appétit!

Ingredients
- 4 cups of organic vegetable broth
- 1 onion, chopped
- 4 ribs celery, chopped
- 2 garlic cloves, minced
- 1 organic zucchini, cubed
- 1 handful fresh kale, chopped
- 1 (15-ounce) can chickpeas, drained and rinsed
- 1 can organic diced tomatoes
- 1 Tablespoon dried parsley
- ½ teaspoon dried thyme
- 1 teaspoon dried oregano
- 1 teaspoon sea salt
- ¼ teaspoon pepper
- Organic Parmesan cheese (optional)

Instructions

Stove Top Method
Combine all ingredients in a large pot. Bring to a boil, then reduce to simmer and cook for 20 minutes or until vegetables are tender. Sprinkle with cheese and serve.

Slow Cook Method
Combine all ingredients except cheese in a crockpot. Cover and let cook on low for 6-8 hours or until vegetables are tender. Sprinkle with cheese and serve.

Notes
- If you do not have vegetable broth on hand, you can substitute any broth that you have.
- You can substitute zucchini with any summer squash.

ENTREES

ASIAN TURKEY WRAPS

 Prep time
5 minutes

 Cook time
15 - 20 minutes

 Servings
3 people

 Dairy-Free, Egg-Free,
Grain-Free, Sugar-Free

I love the flavors of this dish. It reminds me of PF Chang's Chicken Lettuce Wraps.
Although we usually have this for dinner, we've made it ahead of time and taken it
along on picnics and have served it as an appetizer.

Ingredients

- 1 pound ground organic turkey
- 1 cup mushroom caps, chopped
- ½ cup water
- 3 Tablespoon almond/cashew butter
- 1 Tablespoon white vinegar
- 1 (8 ounce) can water chestnuts, drained and chopped
- ½ teaspoon garlic
- ¼ teaspoon ground ginger
- ⅓ cup coconut aminos
- ½ cup green onions (optional)
- 1 head romaine lettuce, separated into leaves

Instructions

1. Cook turkey in skillet about 5 minutes, stirring until turkey crumbles and is no longer pink. Add all ingredients except green onions and lettuce. Cook, stirring frequently, for an additional 5 minutes. Add green onions and cook for an additional minute.
2. Spoon mixture evenly onto lettuce leaves; roll up. Serve with extra aminos if desired.

BALSAMIC CHICKEN

 Prep time
5 minutes

 Cook time
20 minutes

 Servings
4 people

 Dairy-Free, Egg-Free, Nut-Free,
Grain-Free, Sugar-Free

I first made this recipe when I had literally no time for meal prep. I threw the vegetables I had on hand in the pot with some chicken and seasoned it. Who knew it would become one of my husband's favorite dishes?

 Ingredients

- 1 Tablespoon coconut oil
- 1 teaspoon garlic salt
- ½ teaspoon dried basil
- 2 pasture-raised chicken breasts, sliced in half to make 4 thin breasts
- 2 cups mushrooms, sliced
- 2 cups organic bell peppers (any color), sliced
- 1 cup onion, sliced
- ¼ cup balsamic vinegar

 Instructions

1. Heat oil in a skillet over medium heat. Season both sides of the chicken breast with garlic salt. Add chicken to pan.
2. Meanwhile, slice vegetables and add to pan. Pour balsamic vinegar over the chicken and vegetables. Cover and cook for 10 minutes. Remove the lid, flip the chicken and stir the vegetables. Leave the lid off for another 5-10 minutes, or until chicken is cooked completely and vegetables are tender.

BEEF & CRANBERRY SKILLET

 Prep time
10 minutes

 **Cook time**
15 - 20minutes

 **Servings**
4-6 people

 Dairy-Free, Egg-Free, Nut-Free,
Grain-Free, Sugar-Free

This has all of the flavors of a cozy autumn casserole, minus the long oven cook-time. I know the ingredient list looks long, but it's just full of awesome herbs and spices, which make this meal fantastic. Start to finish, the meal takes about 30 minutes, so don't be intimated. Feel free to play around with the spice ratios to make this recipe suit your family's preferences.

Ingredients
- 1 pound free range beef, bison, or venison
- 1 onion, roughly chopped
- 1 organic bell pepper, chopped
- 2 cups mushrooms, chopped
- ¼ cup chopped fresh parsley
- 1 ½ teaspoons Italian seasoning
- ½ teaspoon dried basil
- 1 teaspoon garlic powder
- ½ teaspoon paprika
- ½ teaspoon sea salt
- ¼ teaspoon pepper
- 1 (14 ounce) can organic fire-roasted tomatoes
- 3 Tablespoon balsamic vinegar
- ½ cup whole cranberries (frozen, thawed are fine)
- ½ cup chopped black olives
- 1 (15 ounce) can northern beans, drained and rinsed
- 2 Tablespoons Extra Virgin Olive Oil
- Goat or feta cheese (optional)

Instructions
1. Heat oil in a large skillet over medium heat; cook the meat, onions, peppers and mushrooms for eight to ten minutes, or until meat is browned and cooked through.
2. Season with parsley, Italian seasoning, basil, garlic, paprika, salt and pepper. Add the tomatoes, balsamic vinegar, cranberries, olives, and northern beans. Stir to combine and cook for an additional 10 minutes, or until all vegetables are tender and the flavors are well combined.
3. Drizzle with olive oil and top with goat or feta cheese. Sprinkle with fresh parsley and serve.

CABBAGE ROLLS

 Prep time
5-10 minutes

 Cook time
60 minutes

 Servings
4 people

 Dairy-Free, Nut-Free,
Grain-Free, Sugar-Free

Golabki (AKA Cabbage rolls) is a common Polish cuisine. This is a featured dish for many Polish American families (including ours). Historically, cabbage has always been revered for its medicinal and healing properties. If you're Polish, or if you're not, you're sure to enjoy this epic comfort food.

Ingredients
- 1 pound grass-fed ground beef or bison
- 1 pastured egg
- 1 onion, chopped
- ½ teaspoon sea salt
- ½ teaspoon pepper
- 1 teaspoon garlic powder
- 1 head cabbage
- 2 (15 ounce) cans organic tomato sauce
- 1 (6 ounce) can organic tomato paste

Instructions
1. Preheat oven to 350° F.
2. Boil cabbage for 3 minutes or until leaves are easy to peel off.
3. Mix first six ingredients together in a separate bowl. Add 2 rounded tablespoons of meat mixture inside of a cabbage leaf, and roll. Repeat until all meat mixture is gone. Place small cabbage rolls inside a 9x13 glass baking dish.
4. In a separate bowl, mix tomato sauce and tomato paste together until combined. Pour tomato mixture on top of cabbage rolls. Cover with foil and bake for 1 hour.

SUBSTITUTIONS
- If you have an egg sensitivity, substitute a flax egg. To make a flax egg, mix three tablespoons of water with one tablespoon of ground flax meal. Allow to sit for 5 minutes to gel, then add to the meat mixture.
- If you won't have much time to wait for dinner, you can prepare the cabbage rolls in the morning. Add the uncooked cabbage rolls to a crockpot, cover with the tomato sauce, and allow to cook together on low for 8 hours.

CAULIFLOWER FRIED RICE

| Prep time 10 minutes | Cook time 15 minutes | Servings 2 people | Dairy-Free, Egg-Free, Nut-Free, Grain-Free, Sugar-Free |

Cauliflower is a really cool vegetable. It can be cooked and mashed to replace mashed potatoes, or pulsed in a blender or food processor to replace rice. When I first made this dish, my friends were amazed at how much it resembled the traditional rice they were used to. You can simply use the plain cooked cauliflower rice in any of your favorite dishes that call for rice.

 Ingredients
- 1 head of cauliflower
- 2 pastured eggs (optional)
- 1 cup frozen package of peas
- 1 cup organic red pepper, diced
- 2 Tablespoons coconut aminos
- 3 Tablespoons coconut oil
- ¼ teaspoon ground ginger
- Sea salt to taste

 Instructions
1. Cut cauliflower into florets. In a food processor or blender, process the cauliflower until it forms small "rice" like pieces.
2. In a large pan over medium, add 2 tablespoons of coconut oil. Add in the cauliflower and stir regularly to ensure it doesn't burn.
3. If using eggs, push the cauliflower to the edge of the pan, and crack in the eggs. Stir the eggs as if you're making a scramble. When the eggs are pretty solid, stir into the cauliflower.
4. In a separate pan, add another tablespoon of coconut oil. Cook the red pepper until tender. Add in the peas and cook until warmed. Strain, and add to the cauliflower mixture.
5. Add in coconut aminos, ginger, and sea salt to taste. Cook for two more minutes and then serve.

CHICKEN FAJITAS

 Prep time
5 minutes

 Cook time
15 - 20 minutes

 Servings
2 people

 Dairy-Free, Egg-Free, Nut-Free,
Grain-Free, Sugar-Free

I love Mexican food, but especially fajitas. This is a healthy twist on traditional fajitas. Skip the bleached flour tortilla, add in quality protein and lots of good fats, and you have yourself a meal that primes your body for high performance. Bonus: it's quick and involves limited dishes, making it perfect for busy weeknights.

Ingredients
- 2 pasture-raised chicken breasts, thinly sliced
- 2 Tablespoon coconut oil
- 1 small red onion, thinly sliced
- 2 organic bell peppers, thinly sliced (any color)
- 4 cloves garlic, minced
- 1 teaspoon sea salt
- 1 teaspoon cumin
- 1 teaspoon chili powder
- 1 cup soaked and cooked black beans (or 1 can black beans, drained and rinsed)

Toppings (optional)
- Avocado/fresh guacamole
- Organic Sour Cream
- Raw cheese
- Salsa

Instructions
1. On a medium setting, heat one tablespoon coconut oil in a large skillet. Add chicken breast. Sprinkle with half of salt and garlic and cook until white throughout. Remove chicken and allow to cool on a plate.
2. In the same skillet, add remaining tablespoon of coconut oil. Add sliced bell peppers and onion. Sprinkle the remaining garlic and salt and cook for five minutes
3. Return chicken to skillet with the peppers and onions. Add cumin and chili powder. Stir to combine and cook until veggies reach your desired doneness.
4. In a separate pot, heat the cooked black beans in water until warm. Strain.
5. To serve, place about 1/2 cup black beans on plate and top with fajita mixture. Add your toppings as desired and enjoy.

CHOP SUEY

 Prep time
10 minutes

 Cook time
15 minutes

 Servings
4 people

 Dairy-Free, Egg-Free, Nut-Free,
Grain-Free, Sugar-Free

We make stir-frys all of the time. They are very versatile and different seasonings can be used to change the taste and make a completely unique dish. Try serving your stir-fry over cauliflower rice and/or pair your meal with Egg Drop Soup (page 80).

 Ingredients
- 3 Tablespoons Coconut Aminos
- 1 Tablespoon peeled and grated fresh ginger
- 1 teaspoon arrowroot powder
- ¼ teaspoon crushed red pepper (or to taste)
- 2 cloves garlic, minced
- ¼ cup water
- 1 pound pasture-raised chicken breasts, sliced
- 2 Tablespoons coconut oil
- 1 large sweet onion, cut into thin strips
- 2 organic bell peppers, sliced (any color)
- 2 cups of vegetables of choice (broccoli, mushrooms, celery, bean sprouts, etc.)

 Instructions
1. In a small bowl, whisk aminos, ginger, arrowroot powder, red pepper, garlic, and water. Set aside
2. In a large skillet, warm one tablespoon coconut oil over medium-high heat. Add chicken and cook until meat is no longer pink and cooked throughout, about 5 minutes. Remove to plate.
3. Add remaining tablespoon of coconut oil to skillet. Add peppers, onions and vegetables of choice, and stir-fry for 5 minutes. (Add 1-2 tablespoons of water if skillet is dry).
4. Pour stir-fry sauce over vegetables. Return chicken to skillet and stir to combine. Simmer for 3-5 minutes.
5. Serve alone, or over cauliflower rice.

Notes
- Use ⅛ teaspoon ground ginger instead of fresh ginger.
- Use ¼ teaspoon garlic powder instead of fresh garlic.

COCONUT CHICKEN NUGGETS

 Prep time
10 minutes

 Cook time
20 minutes

 Servings
4 people

 Dairy-Free, Grain-Free,
Sugar-Free

If your kids love chicken nuggets, then they will love this recipe. Nearly all frozen or fast food nuggets contain ingredients that harm your body. These nuggets taste great and contain ingredients that nourish your body, like the super food coconut. Bonus: they are easy to pick up and eat with your fingers, making them perfect for children.

 Ingredients
- 1 pound pasture-raised chicken, ground
- 1 teaspoon onion powder
- ½ teaspoon garlic powder
- ¼ teaspoon paprika
- ¼ teaspoon sea salt
- ¼ teaspoon pepper
- ¾ cup almond flour, separated
- ½ cup unsweetened shredded coconut
- ½ cup coconut oil

Instructions
1. Preheat oven to 375° F.
2. In a bowl combine, 1/2 cup almond flour and shredded coconut. Mix to combine.
3. In a separate bowl, combine the ground chicken, 1/4 cup almond flour, onion powder, garlic powder, paprika, sea salt, and pepper. Mix well until everything is incorporated.
4. In a sauté pan, melt coconut oil on medium heat. Roll about 2 tablespoons of chicken mixture into a ball. Coat with the coconut and almond mixture. Repeat with the remaining chicken.
5. Place half of the nuggets into heated coconut oil and cook on each side for about 3 to 4 minutes. Transfer nuggets to a parchment lined bake pan. Repeat with the remaining nuggets.
6. When all chicken nuggets have been browned, place bake pan in the oven for 5-8 minutes to allow the chicken to cook through. Allow the nuggets to cool and serve.

 Notes
If you have an almond allergy, try grinding your own nut flours with cashews, Brazil nuts, macadamia nuts, or hazelnuts.

CREAMY ARTICHOKE CHICKEN

 Prep time
5 minutes

 Cook time
40 minutes

 Servings
4 people

 Egg-Free, Nut-Free,
Grain-Free, Sugar-Free

If you like spinach artichoke dip, then you'll adore this recipe. Although easy to prepare, this dish is delivers impressive flavor and a beautiful presentation.

 Ingredients

- 4 pasture-raised chicken breasts
- 4-5 (2 cups) organic tomatoes, cored and chopped
- 1 can (14 ounce) of artichoke hearts, drained and chopped
- 10 ounce frozen spinach, thawed and drained
- 2 teaspoon arrowroot powder
- 1 cup Grapeseed Vegenaise
- ½ cup organic mozzarella cheese, shredded
- ½ cup organic Parmesan, shredded
- 1 teaspoon garlic powder
- Salt and pepper to taste.

 Instructions

1. Preheat oven to 350° F. Place chicken breasts in a 9x13 glass dish.
2. Combine tomatoes, artichoke hearts, spinach, arrowroot powder, vegenaise, cheeses, and garlic in a medium bowl and toss to combine. Add salt and pepper to taste.
3. Spread the tomato/spinach mixture over the chicken breasts. Place in the oven and bake for 40 minutes, or until chicken is no longer pink.
4. Remove from oven and serve.

EASY BROILED MAHI MAHI

 Prep time
5 minutes

 Cook time
14-16 minutes

 Servings
2 people

 Dairy-Free, Egg-Free, Nut-Free, Grain-Free, Sugar-Free

Skip the fried fish, and opt for this quick and simple baked version.

 Ingredients
- 1 pound wild-caught Mahi Mahi fillets
- ¼ cup Grapeseed Vegenaise
- ¼ cup salsa
- 2 Tablespoons lemon juice
- ¼ teaspoon dried basil
- ¼ teaspoon pepper
- ¼ teaspoon garlic salt

 Instructions
1. Preheat your oven's broiler.
2. In a small bowl, mix together the vegenaise, salsa, lemon juice, basil, pepper, and garlic salt.
3. Arrange fillets in a single layer in a glass baking dish. Spoon vegenaise mixture over each filet, making sure to completely cover the fish.
4. Broil 8-inches away from the heat until cooked through (about 14-16 minutes).

 Notes
If fish begins to brown before it is cooked, cover with foil.

EGGPLANT AND LAMB RAGU

 Prep time
10 minutes

 Cook time
30 minutes

 Servings
4 people

 Dairy-Free, Egg-Free, Nut-Free,
Grain-Free, Sugar-Free

Not only is the color beautiful, but it has big flavors that will knock your socks off. The dish is permeated with a nice grass-fed lamb flavor, not at all strong but delightful, set off perfectly by the herbs and spices.

Ingredients
- 2 eggplants (about 2 pounds)
- 3 Tablespoons coconut oil
- 1 teaspoon sea salt
- 1 ½ pounds lean ground lamb
- 2 onions, chopped
- 4 cloves garlic, minced
- 1 Tablespoon dried oregano
- 1 teaspoon cinnamon
- ½ teaspoon pepper
- 1 (28 ounce) can organic crushed tomatoes
- 1 cup organic beef broth (bonus: use bone broth)
- 1 Tablespoon rice wine vinegar

Instructions
1. Peel and cube eggplants into one inch chunks. Toss with 2 tablespoons coconut oil and ¼ teaspoon salt. Broil on greased baking sheet for 8 to 10 minutes. Remove from oven.
2. Meanwhile, in a large pan, heat remaining tablespoon of coconut oil over medium heat. Brown lamb for 10 minutes, or until no longer pink. Strain meat and return it to the pot.
3. Add remaining ingredients and roasted eggplant to the pot. Stir to combine. Cover and cook on medium to low heat for 10 minutes.

Notes
- You may substitute ground grass-fed beef or bison.
- If you have homemade canned stewed or diced tomatoes, those work as a replacement for the crushed tomatoes.

PAPRIKA CHICKEN

 Prep time
5 - 10 minutes

 Cook time
20 minutes

 Servings
2 people

 Egg-Free, Nut-Free,
Grain-Free, Sugar-Free

There are many weeknights when I'm too tired to cook. That's when easy and quick recipes like this one come in handy. But don't underestimate it just because it's simple; it's full of flavor and tossed in a delicious creamy sauce.

 Ingredients

- 2 pasture-raised chicken breasts, cut into bite size pieces
- 2 organic bell peppers, cut into large chunks
- 1 Tablespoon coconut oil
- 8 ounces mushrooms, sliced
- ½ teaspoon sea salt
- 1 teaspoon minced garlic
- ½ teaspoon pepper
- 2 teaspoons paprika
- ¾ cup organic sour cream
- 2 Tablespoons grass-fed butter

 Instructions

1. In a large skillet, sauté bell peppers in the coconut oil over medium heat. Add mushrooms and peppers, and cook until just tender. Remove the vegetables from the pan.
2. Add the chicken to the skillet. Brown the chicken until white throughout. Season the chicken with salt, pepper, garlic, and paprika. Return the vegetables to the skillet and add the butter. Continue cooking until the butter is melted.
3. Turn down the heat to low and add the sour cream. Stir until melted, making sure to scrape the bottom of the skillet and get all the flavors mixed into the sour cream.

SLOPPY JOES

 Prep time
5 minutes

 Cook time
10 minutes

 Servings
4 people

 Dairy-Free, Egg-Free, Nut-Free,
Grain-Free, Sugar-Free

Sloppy Joes are a kid-friendly meal that can be quickly prepared for lunch or dinner. It's also a great meal to make in bulk and serve at a party. This recipe is free of high fructose corn syrup and full of high quality meat.

Ingredients

- 1 pound ground grass fed beef/bison
- ½ cup onion, diced
- ½ teaspoon garlic powder
- ½ teaspoon sea salt
- ¼ teaspoon black pepper
- ¾ cup xylitol sweetened ketchup
- 1 Tablespoon Tabasco sauce (Frank's)
- 1 Tablespoon mustard
- 2 teaspoon lemon juice
- 1 head of lettuce (Boston, Romaine, Butter or Iceberg)

Instructions

1. Begin browning ground meat in a large frying pan over medium heat.
2. Meanwhile, chop onion and add to pan.
3. When the meat is cooked and onions are tender, strain the fat off of the meat.
4. Return meat to pan. Season meat with salt, pepper, and garlic and stir to mix completely.
5. Add ketchup, tabasco sauce, mustard, and lemon juice. Stir and continue cooking until warmed through.
6. To serve, spoon several tablespoons of the mixture into the center of a lettuce leaf, taco style.

Notes

To make this meal more affordable, cut your meat with sprouted and cooked lentils.

SPAGHETTI & MEATBALLS

 Prep time
15 minutes

 Cook time
60 minutes

 Servings
4 people

 Nut-Free, Grain-Free,
Sugar-Free

Pasta has always been one of my favorite meals. My husband used to joke that I made noodles with every meal. Now I make spaghetti squash, top it with sauce and meatballs, and I don't even miss the noodles.

Ingredients
- 1 pound prepared meatballs *(page 58)*
- 1 spaghetti squash

Sauce
- 1 Tablespoon grapeseed oil
- ½ Tablespoon minced garlic
- ¼ cup diced onion
- 2 cans (15 ounce) organic tomato sauce
- 1 can (14.5 ounce) organic diced tomatoes
- ¼ teaspoon pepper
- ¾ teaspoon sea salt
- 1 teaspoon Italian seasoning
- 1 teaspoon parsley
- ½ teaspoon oregano
- Dash of red pepper
- Dash of xylitol

Instructions
1. Preheat oven to 350°F . Place whole spaghetti squash in oven for 45 minutes to 1 hour, or until the squash can be easily pierced by a fork.
2. Meanwhile, in a medium-large saucepan, add oil, garlic, and onion. Cook over medium heat until onions are translucent and begin to brown. Add the remaining sauce ingredients and stir to combine. Bring to a boil, then reduce to simmer and allow to cook for at least 10 minutes.
3. When the squash is cooked through, carefully remove from oven and place on cutting board. Cut the squash lengthwise and spoon out the seeds. Using a fork, scrape out the squash "noodles" and place in a bowl. Top with meatballs and sauce. Garnish with parsley or Parmesan cheese.

SUBSTITUTIONS
In a time crunch? Skip making the meatballs, and just cook ground beef/bison with the garlic and onion in the saucepan. Brown the meat until cooked through, and then add the remaining ingredients.

SWEET POTATO SLIDERS

 Prep time
5-10 minutes

 Cook time
40 minutes

 Servings
4 people

 Dairy-Free, Egg-Free, Nut-Free,
Grain-Free, Sugar-Free

Many restaurants are getting on board with offering lettuce wraps or gluten-free buns. But even gluten-free breads are starchy and full of sugar. These sliders replace the starchy buns with sweet potato slices.

 Ingredients
- 1 large sweet potato
- 1 large yellow onion, sliced
- 1 pound ground bison
- 1 organic tomato, sliced
- Romaine lettuce leaves
- Grapeseed oil
- Sea salt and pepper, to taste

 Instructions
1. Preheat oven to 350° F. Line a baking sheet with unbleached parchment paper. Wash sweet potato well and pat dry. Slice sweet potatoes cross-wise into even round discs. Brush the sweet potatoes with a little bit of grapeseed oil. Season with sea salt and pepper. Bake for 40 minutes, or until easily pierced with a fork.
2. Make burger patties to match the size of your sweet potato discs. Season to taste and grill or cook them to desired doneness.
3. Assemble your sliders in this order: 1 sweet potato, 1 burger patty, 1 onion disc, 1 tomato slice, 1 piece of lettuce, condiments of choice, and 1 sweet potato.

DESSERTS

APPLE CRUMBLE

Prep time	 Cook time	Servings	 Egg-Free, Grain-Free,
10 minutes	25-30 minutes	4 people	Sugar-Free

Warm apple crisp is delicious all year around, but especially in the fall when the apples are in full season. Most fruit crisps are loaded with brown sugar, white flour, and oats. After many attempts, I finally got this green apple crumble just how I want it. This dessert will make your kitchen smell divine and will have you coming back for seconds.

Ingredients

- 5 cups organic granny smith apples, peeled and sliced
- 1 teaspoon cinnamon
- 3 Tablespoon xylitol, separated
- 1 Tablespoon arrowroot powder
- ¾ cup almond flour
- ½ cup chopped pecans or walnuts
- 1 teaspoon vanilla extract
- 2 Tablespoon grass-fed butter, softened

Instructions

1. Preheat oven to 375°F.
2. In a large bowl, toss apples, cinnamon and one tablespoon of xylitol. Pour into an 8x8 baking dish.
3. Using the same bowl, stir together the remaining ingredients until well combined and crumbly. Sprinkle the topping on the apple mixture.
4. Bake for 25-30 minutes, or until apples are soft and topping is golden brown.

Notes

If you have a dairy sensitivity, you can replace the butter with ghee or coconut oil. You may also try substituting berries for the apples for an exciting new dessert option.

CASHEW BUTTER BALLS

 Prep time
5 minutes

 Cook time
15-20 minutes

 Servings
10 balls

 Dairy-Free, Egg-Free,
Grain-Free, Sugar-Free

I've never been a huge candy eater, but one thing I could never resist was Reese's Peanut Butter Eggs at Easter. However, knowing what I know now about how the body works, I avoid those and avoid putting them in my children's Easter baskets. However, that doesn't mean I need to avoid the perfect combination of nut butter and chocolate. In my opinion, those are two flavors that were destined to be together. Hope you enjoy these Cashew Butter Balls as much as I do.

 Ingredients
- ½ cup cashew butter
- 2 Tablespoons coconut flour
- 1 teaspoon xylitol
- ½ teaspoon vanilla extract
- ⅓ cup Lily's Dark Chocolate Chips

 Instructions
1. Line a baking sheet with parchment paper and set aside.
2. Combine all ingredients except chocolate chips in a bowl. Form into 1" balls.
3. In a small saucepan (or double boiler), melt chocolate chips over low heat, stirring frequently. Coat each cashew butter ball in chocolate and place on the baking sheet.
4. Refrigerate 15-20 minutes before serving.

Notes
You can use any raw, unsweetened nut butter in this recipe.

CHOCOLATE COCONUT
MOUSSE

Prep time 2-3 minutes	Cook time 0 minutes	Servings 2 people	Dairy-Free, Egg-Free, Nut-Free, Grain-Free, Sugar-Free

My husband grew up having dessert or a snack every evening, so almost immediately following dinner, he asks, "What's for dessert?" This is by far the quickest dessert we make, and is my "go-to" on the nights I don't feel up for baking.

 Ingredients

- 1 can organic coconut milk
- 2 Tablespoons cocoa powder
- ¼ teaspoon vanilla extract
- Stevia, to taste

 Instructions

1. Place coconut milk in the refrigerator for a few hours or in the freezer for an hour so that the cream hardens, separates and rises to the top. Open the can and scoop out the hardened cream, placing it in a large mixing bowl. Reserve the liquid at the bottom of the can for a smoothie at a later time.
2. Use a mixer to slowly whip the coconut cream. Add cocoa, stevia and vanilla extract and gradually work to a higher speed until ingredients are well combined and you have incorporated enough air for desired texture.
3. Top with your favorite variety nuts, berries, or unsweetened coconut flakes. Or, you can dip strawberries in it for a "chocolate covered strawberry" flavor. Mousse will keep in the refrigerator for several days.

COCONUT WATER POPSICLES

 Prep time
5 minutes

 Cook time
7 minutes to 5 hours,
depending on mold

 Servings

 Dairy-Free, Egg-Free, Nut-Free,
Grain-Free, Sugar-Free

Kids (and adults) love popsicles, especially on a hot summer afternoon. But many popsicles are full of artificial flavors, colors, and sugars. These coconut water popsicles are refreshing and easy to prepare ahead of time. My daughter loves making these (and eating them).

 Ingredients
- Berries & kiwi, sliced or diced, fresh or frozen
- Coconut Water

Fill popsicle molds ¾ of the way with fruit. Pour coconut water into molds until filled. Place molds in freezer. Allow popsicles to freeze completely before serving. Time will vary depending on your popsicle mold. Once your popsicles are ready to serve, run the bottom of the popsicle molds under warm water to help release them from the molds.

 Notes
- If you do not have a popsicle mold, you can use paper cups and popsicle sticks.
- Zoku popsicle molds can freeze your popsicles in as little as 7 minutes.

GRAIN FREE
ZUCCHINI MUFFINS

 Prep time
7-10 minutes

 Cook time
25 minutes

 Servings
12 muffins

 Dairy-Free, Grain-Free,
Sugar-Free

One of my favorite breads from childhood was my mom's zucchini bread. It didn't even taste like vegetables, largely because of the three cups of white sugar. We've adapted this recipe to fit our healthier lifestyle and I can say that it's an even better way to eat your vegetables. Packed with protein, good oils, and grated zucchini, you can eat them guilt-free anytime of the day.

Ingredients
- 2 cups almond flour
- ½ teaspoon sea salt
- ½ teaspoon baking soda
- ¼ teaspoon cream of tartar
- 1 teaspoon ground cinnamon
- 1 teaspoon pumpkin pie spice
- ¼ cup xylitol
- ¼ cup Grapeseed oil
- 2 pastured eggs
- 1 cup grated zucchini
- ½ cup pecans, coarsely chopped

Instructions
1. Preheat oven to 350°F. Grease 12 muffin pan with coconut oil or line with cupcake liners.
2. In a large bowl, combine almond flour, salt, baking soda, cream of tartar, cinnamon, pumpkin pie spice, and xylitol.
3. In a medium bowl, whisk together eggs and Grapeseed oil.
4. Blend the almond mixture into the wet ingredients until thoroughly combined. Then, fold in the zucchini and pecans.
5. Bake for 25 minutes, or until a knife inserted into the center of a muffin comes out clean. Let the muffins cool in the pans for 15 minutes, then serve.

Notes
- Grated zucchini can be substituted with 1 cup peeled and grated green apple.
- Grapeseed oil can be substituted with coconut oil.

HOMEMADE ICE CREAM

 Prep time
2 minutes

 Cook time
30 minutes

 Servings
4 people

 Egg-Free, Nut-Free,
Grain-Free, Sugar-Free

This creamy, frozen treat is easier to prep than you may think. It's the perfect dessert to serve at a birthday party or summer picnic.

 Ingredients
- 2 cups organic whole milk
- 1 cup coconut cream (skim the solid part off of a can of coconut milk)
- ¼ cup xylitol
- ½ Tablespoon pure vanilla extract

 Instructions
1. Blend all ingredients together until combined.
2. Pour mixture into your ice cream maker. Process your ice cream according to your maker's instructions. Time will vary depending on your ice cream maker.

 Notes
- You can make this dairy-free by using 2 full cans of coconut milk instead of the raw milk and coconut cream.
- You can also add other ingredients to this recipe, such as cocoa powder, frozen berries, peppermint and Lily's Dark Chocolate Chips, etc.
- We use the Cuisinart ice cream maker, and it takes approximately 30 minutes to produce ice cream.

MINI-CHEESECAKES

 Prep time
15 minutes

 Cook time
50-55 minutes

 Servings
20 mini-cheesecakes

 Grain-Free,
Sugar-Free

Cheesecake is one of life's simple pleasures. By making this with quality dairy, you'll be delivering a dessert that's rich in flavor and good fats. Go ahead – indulge!

CRUST

Ingredients
- 1 ½ cups almond flour
- 3 Tablespoon grass-fed butter, melted
- 1 teaspoon Stevia

 Instructions
1. Heat oven to 350° F. Line muffin pans with cupcake liners.
2. Melt the butter. Mix the ingredients together and pat into liners with your fingers.
3. Bake for about 10 minutes or until the crust is beginning to brown.
   Start checking after 8 minutes because once it starts to brown, it goes quickly.

CHEESECAKE

Ingredients
- 8 ounces organic cream cheese, softened
- 1 cup organic sour cream
- 4 pastured eggs, beaten
- ½ cup xylitol
- 1 Tablespoon pure vanilla extract

 Instructions
1. Beat cream cheese until smooth. Mix in remaining ingredients. Pour cheese mixture on top of the almond crust.
2. Bake at 350° F for 40-45 minutes or until center is set. Remove from oven.
3. Let the mini-cheesecakes cool for 15 minutes before putting them into the refrigerator. Refrigerate for one hour before serving.

 Notes
For extra credit, top your cheesecakes with this Very Berry Sauce *(page 172).*

PUMPKIN CHOCOLATE CHIP COOKIES

 Prep time
10 minutes

 Cook time
8- 9 minutes

 Servings
24 cookies

 Dairy-Free, Grain-Free,
Sugar-Free

The taste of fall shines in this recipe. Take pumpkin, pair it with dark chocolate, and you have one irresistible cookie.

 Ingredients

- 2 cups almond flour
- 1 teaspoon baking soda
- 1 teaspoon cinnamon
- ½ cup Lily's Dark Chocolate Chips
- ¼ cup xylitol
- ⅓ cup coconut oil, slightly melted
- 1 Tablespoon pure vanilla extract
- 1 pastured egg
- ⅓ cup pumpkin puree

 Instructions

1. Preheat oven to 350° F.
2. In a mixer, combine all ingredients except the chocolate chips. Mix on low speed until well combined. Stir in the chocolate chips with a spatula.
3. Spoon onto cookie sheets lined with unbleached parchment paper. Drop them in about 1 tablespoon measures about 2 inches apart (a mini ice cream scoop works great). Then, slightly flattened the cookies with the back side of a spoon.
4. Bake 8-9 minutes. After removing them from the oven, gently transferred the cookies to the cooling rack by sliding the parchment paper right off the cookie sheet onto the cooling rack.

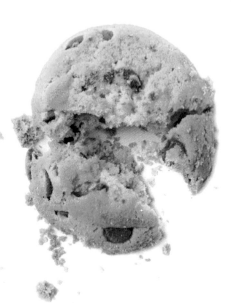

RED VELVET CAKE

Prep time 15 minutes	 Cook time 30-40 minutes	 Servings 10-14 cake piece	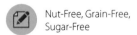 Nut-Free, Grain-Free, Sugar-Free

There are occasions when you just want a fancy cake (birthdays and anniversaries) That's when I make this cake. Although it takes a bit of time, the person you're making it for will certainly thank you.

Ingredients

- ½ cup grass-fed butter
- 9 pastured eggs
- ⅔ cup xylitol
- 1 Tablespoon pure vanilla extract
- ½ cup plain yogurt or sour cream

- 1 Tablespoon natural red food coloring
- ¾ cup sifted coconut flour
- ½ teaspoon sea salt
- 1 teaspoon aluminum-free baking powder
- 2 Tablespoons unsweetened cocoa powder

Instructions

1. Preheat oven to 350°F. Set out butter and eggs and bring to room temperature. Prepare two 8" cake pans by greasing with non-hydrogenated shortening and dusting with extra cocoa powder. Tap pans on all sides to distribute cocoa powder in an even layer.
2. Whisk eggs in a bowl until foamy, and add vanilla extract. Set aside. In a second bowl, combine coconut flour, sea salt, baking powder, and cocoa powder.
3. In a mixer, whisk butter for about 30 seconds to make it fluffy. Add xylitol in a steady stream and cream together for 2 minutes, scraping the sides of the bowl occasionally. Beat until light and fluffy. Slowly stream in beaten eggs, beating continuously. Then add in dry ingredients and mix until combined.
4. Bake for 30-40 minutes, or until batter is set and springs back when touched. Cover top with foil and bake longer if center is not set. Remove cake from oven and allow to cool for 10 minutes.
5. Invert pans onto a cookie sheet and let cool completely. Transfer 1 cake layer to a serving dish. Frost cake with cream cheese frosting. Add top layer to cake and cover completely with frosting.
6. Store in the refrigerator. Cake tastes best when served at room temperature.

CREAM CHEESE FROSTING

This basic cream cheese frosting can be used on cookies, cupcakes, or layered cakes.

Ingredients

- 2 (8-ounce) packages organic cream cheese
- ½ cup xylitol

- 1 teaspoon arrowroot powder
- 1 stick (8 Tablespoons) grass-fed butter
- 1 teaspoon pure vanilla extract

Instructions

1. Bring cream cheese and butter to room temperature.
2. In a blender, combine xylitol and arrowroot powder on high speed until xylitol resembles powdered sugar.
3. Using a mixer, blend cream cheese until smooth and creamy, then add powdered xylitol and beat for about 2 minutes. Beat in butter and vanilla just until smooth and incorporated.

BEVERAGES

AVOCADO SHAKE

 Prep time
5 minutes

 Cook time
0 minutes

 Servings
1 person

 Dairy-Free, Egg-Free,
Grain-Free, Sugar-Free

We were originally introduced to this drink by a Brazilian friend of ours. In her country, avocados are plentiful, and avocado shakes are very popular. This three-ingredient smoothie is packed with protein and good fats, making a very satisfying treat.

 Ingredients
- ½ ripe haas avocado
- 2 cup almond/cashew/coconut milk
- Stevia or xylitol to taste

 Instructions
Place all ingredients in blender and blend until smooth!

BRAIN BOOSTING LATTE

 **Prep time**
3-5 minutes

 Cook time
1 minutes

 Servings
1 people

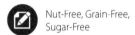 **Nut-Free, Grain-Free, Sugar-Free**

Mmm…coffee! There are few things I like more than sipping on this frothy cup of coffee first thing in the morning. By blending in these good fats, you are supporting your brain and nervous system. Add in the egg yolk and you have breakfast in a mug.

 Ingredients
- ½ cup organic Half & Half
- 1 ½ – 2 Tablespoons grass-fed butter
- 8 ounces low-acid organic coffee, freshly brewed
- 1 pastured egg yolk (optional)
- Xylitol or stevia to taste (optional)

 Instructions
1. In a small saucepan on low heat, slightly warm the half and half on the stove. Do not heat till steaming otherwise you'll denature the fats and proteins.
2. Meanwhile, brew coffee and add to blender.
3. Add butter, half & half, egg yolk and xylitol to the coffee in the blender. Blend all ingredients on low for 20 seconds.

 Notes
Omit the egg if you're sensitive to them. If you cannot have dairy, substitute ghee or MCT oil for the butter and a milk substitute (almond, cashew, or coconut) for the half and half.

CHIA TEA

 Prep time
2 minutes

 Cook time
7 minutes

 Servings
4 people

 Dairy-Free, Egg-Free,
Grain-Free, Sugar-Free

This spiced milk tea originates in India but has become quite popular in recent years. Many chai teas contain hydrogenated oils and loads of sugar. This recipe removes all of the harmful ingredients and retains all of the delicious flavors of this aromatic tea.

 Ingredients
- 2 cups filtered water
- 2 black tea bags
- 1 cinnamon stick
- 6 cardamom pods, crushed (or 1/8 teaspoon ground)
- 1 whole clove
- ¼ teaspoon ground ginger
- 2 cups unsweetened almond milk
- 1 Tablespoon grass-fed butter or MCT oil
- ¼ cup xylitol (or to taste)
- Ground cinnamon for sprinkling (optional)

 Instructions
1. In a small saucepan, combine the first 6 ingredients. Bring to a boil. Reduce heat; cover and simmer for 5 minutes. Strain into a medium saucepan.
2. Pour xylitol into tea mixture and stir until combined. Stir in milk and warm until heated through. Pour into mugs and top with a dash of cinnamon or a cinnamon stick.

Note
Try playing around with the type of milk you like in here. If xylitol does not sit well with you, try sweetening your tea with liquid stevia to taste.

EGGNOG

 Prep time
3-5 minutes

 Cook time
0 minutes

 Servings
10 people

 Nut-Free, Grain-Free,
Sugar-Free

Christmas is my favorite time of the year for many reasons. It's a tradition in my family to make this delicious treat while we decorate the family Christmas tree. I've adapted my mom's famous eggnog recipe to fit our healthier lifestyle.

Ingredients
- 6 pastured eggs
- 1 teaspoon vanilla
- ½ teaspoon sea salt
- 2 pints organic half & half
- 2 pints organic heavy whipping cream
- ¼ cup xylitol
- Nutmeg for sprinkling

 ### Instructions
1. Place all ingredients in a blender. Blend on low speed until well incorporated.
2. Pour into glasses and sprinkle with nutmeg.

GREEN SMOOTHIE

 Prep time
1-2 minutes

 Cook time
0 minutes

 Servings
1 people

 Dairy-Free, Egg-Free, Nut-Free,
Grain-Free, Sugar-Free

Getting enough green, leafy vegetables into our diets is difficult for most people, especially picky eaters. Hiding spinach in a smoothie is an easy way to incorporate more greens into your (and your children's) diet.

 Ingredients
- 1 cup coconut water
- 4 frozen strawberries
- ⅓ cup frozen blueberries
- 2 cups fresh spinach

 Instructions
Blend all ingredients together until smooth. Serve immediately.

TRIPLE BERRY BLAST

 Prep time
2-3 minutes

 Cook time
0 minutes

 Servings
2 people

 Dairy-Free, Egg-Free, Nut-Free,
Grain-Free, Sugar-Free

Smoothies are the best way to get a mega-dose of vitamins and antioxidants at anytime of the day. We love making smoothies in the morning because they are a quick and portable option.

 Ingredients
- ½ cup organic raspberries (fresh or frozen)
- ½ cup organic blueberries (fresh or frozen)
- ½ cup organic strawberries (fresh or frozen)
- 1 cup ice (do not use if using frozen berries)
- ½ teaspoon Stevia
- 2 cups water

 Instructions
Blend all ingredients together until smooth. Serve immediately.

Notes
You can use any ratio of berries that you have on hand. For example, if you only have strawberries, use 1 ½ cups of strawberries.

WHEY COOL CHOCOLATE SHAKE

 Prep time 1-2 minutes	Cook time 0 minutes	Servings 1 people	Egg-Free, Grain-Free, Sugar-Free

Running low on time? Don't skip a meal. Instead, make this shake and take it with you. If we are traveling, we'll bring the protein powder and a blender bottle. Then we can make this shake anytime, anywhere.

 Ingredients
- 2 cups almond, cashew or coconut milk
- 1 scoop Whey Cool Chocolate Protein

 Instructions
Blend until smooth and enjoy.

 Notes
If you're like me, I get bored with the "same old, same old". To add some variety to this simple but delicious shake, try adding one or more of the following:
1 Tablespoon chia seeds, 1 handful of organic berries, 1 handful of organic spinach, or ½ avocado.

SAUCES & DRESSINGS

AZ FRY SAUCE

| Prep time 2-3 minutes | Cook time 0 minutes | Servings 1 cup | Dairy-Free, Egg-Free, Nut-Free, Grain-Free, Sugar-Free |

Add some pizzazz to your favorite burger with this sauce. I originally designed it for fries but find myself eating it on everything. Serve this sauce with Butternut Squash Fries (page 50), Sweet Potato Sliders (page 122), or Coconut Chicken Nuggets (page 108).

Ingredients
- ¼ cup Grapeseed Vegenaise
- ½ cup xylitol sweetened ketchup
- 2 Tablespoons Extra Virgin Olive Oil
- 1 teaspoon raw apple cider vinegar
- 2 teaspoons yellow mustard
- ½ teaspoon garlic powder
- ¼ teaspoon onion powder
- Dash of cayenne pepper (more if you like it spicy)
- Sea salt and pepper to taste

Instructions
Whisk all ingredients together until combined.

BALSAMIC VINAIGRETTE

 Prep time
2-3 minutes

 Cook time
0 minutes

 Servings
2 cup

 Dairy-Free, Egg-Free, Nut-Free, Grain-Free, Sugar Free

Why get store-bought dressings, filled with hydrogenated oils and sugars, when you can whip up this dressing in under five minutes? Top your salad greens with a delicious "good for you" dressing. This balsamic vinaigrette is simple and savory.

Ingredients
- 1 ½ cups balsamic vinegar
- 2 Tablespoons fresh lemon juice
- 6 Tablespoons Dijon mustard
- 2 Tablespoons onion, finely diced
- 1 teaspoon dried basil
- ¼ cup extra virgin olive oil
- Black pepper to taste

Instructions
Blend all ingredients for 10-20 seconds. Store in the refrigerator.

PEPPER DRESSING

 Prep time
2-3 minutes

 Cook time
3 minutes

 Servings
1 1/2 cups

 Dairy-Free, Egg-Free, Nut-Free,
Grain-Free, Sugar-Free

The pepper is bold but not too sharp in this dressing that will complement your favorite salad ingredients. It's easy to mix up and great to have on hand.

 Ingredients
- ¼ cup xylitol
- ½ cup vinegar
- 3 teaspoon sea salt
- 4 teaspoon black pepper
- ¾ cup extra virgin olive oil

 Instructions
1. Heat the first four ingredients in a saucepan over medium heat. Stir constantly until xylitol is dissolved.
2. Remove from heat and stir in olive oil.
3. Refrigerate for one our before serving.

POPPY SEED DRESSING

 Prep time
7 minutes

 Cook time
0 minutes

 Servings
1 ½ cups

 Dairy-Free, Egg-Free, Nut-Free,
Grain-Free, Sugar-Free

This homemade poppy seed dressing uses simple ingredients and takes hardly any time to make. I love serving this tangy-sweet dressing over salad greens or fresh fruit.

 Ingredients
- ½ cup xylitol
- 1 ½ teaspoon onion salt
- 1 teaspoon ground mustard
- ⅓ cup white vinegar
- 1 cup grapeseed oil
- 1 Tablespoon poppy seeds

 Instructions
1. In a mixer, combine sugar, onion salt, mustard and vinegar. Mix well.
2. Gradually add oil while beating on medium speed. Beat for 5 minutes or until very thick. Stir in poppy seeds.
3. Cover and refrigerate.

THAI GINGER
LIME MARINADE

|  Prep time
2-3 minutes | Cook time
0 minutes | Servings
3/4 cup | Dairy-Free, Egg-Free, Nut-Free,
Grain-Free, Sugar Free |

This marinade is great with Thai-Ginger Bacon Wrapped Water Chestnuts (page 62) or with chicken breasts.

 Ingredients
- ¼ cup Coconut Aminos
- ¼ cup Extra Virgin Olive Oil
- 2 Tablespoons fresh lime juice
- 1 lime zest
- 2 Tablespoons grated fresh ginger
- ½ teaspoon pepper
- 1 clove minced garlic

 Instructions
Whisk the above ingredients until combined.

 Notes
If you do not have fresh ginger, you can substitute 1/4 teaspoon ground ginger.
If you do not have fresh garlic, you can substitute 1/8 teaspoon ground garlic

VERY BERRY SAUCE

 Prep time
5 minutes

 Cook time
10 minutes

 Servings
about 1 cup

 Dairy-Free, Egg-Free, Nut-Free, Grain-Free, Sugar-Free

Enjoy this sauce on ice cream, yogurt, cottage cheese, Almond Flour Waffles (page 18), and Mini Cheesecakes (page 138). You can use any fresh or frozen berries you have on hand.

 Ingredients
- 4 cups organic berries (strawberries, blueberries, raspberries, blackberries)
- ¼ cup xylitol

 Instructions
1. Clean berries and remove any stems. Place berries and xylitol in a small saucepan. Bring to a boil, then reduce heat and cook 5 minutes until syrupy and berries soften and break down.
2. For a chunky sauce, smash with a fork. For a smoother sauce, transfer to a food processor or blender and process until smooth.

 Notes
If you are using frozen berries, your cook time will be longer. If you'd like to thicken your sauce, you can whisk in 1 teaspoon of arrowroot powder at a time until it reaches your desired consistency.

Made in the USA
Middletown, DE
21 February 2017